GUNNER

a beagle's story

GUNNER

a beagle's story

Mark T. Harter

Let it Beagle Media

Let it Beagle Media
Hilton, NY 14468
gunnerthebeagle.com

Gunner, a beagle's story
Written by Mark T. Harter
Edited by Andrea Hicks

All photos by Mark T. Harter, Tracy Harter, and Mia Harter. Cover based in part on a photo by Patty Coffee (used with permission).

ISBN 979-8-9883001-1-3 (Hardcover)
ISBN 979-8-9883001-2-0 (Paperback)
Library of Congress Control Number: 2023908288
LIBM-B1-1.0

1st Edition
1st Printing June 2023

Disclaimer- this book is based in part or in whole on events of the life of Gunner and Mark T. Harter. Names within are based wholly or in part on actual persons and for most part depicts their time together in as true a telling as possible.

To Gunner, the journey
was the reward.

INTRODUCTION

As I begin to write this, it's been twenty four hours unlike any other in my life. In addition to everything that has happened to me, these last few days are too numerous to count? My daughter having surgery that we have been working towards for close to seven years, Gunner, and my mother in the hospital? It's safe to say its been a week different than any other.

That's jumping ahead. Most of that is not what this story is about: it's about dogs, namely one beloved dog named Gunner the beagle that we adopted as a senior from a shelter. But that is likewise jumping ahead.

Dogs. They have been with us for countless millennial. But what are they really? A dog is a wolf. They might not look like one, or act like their still wild cousins, but at their core, a wolf. That seems simple to say but when understanding dogs it's always important to keep two things in mind: they are essentially wolves, and to a dog, everything in their world is experienced by smell rather than sight. Once that is understood, a dog's behavior makes sense.

Humankind and dogs (wolves) association goes back millennia. I think it's fairly safe to say that had those first wolves not overcome their fear of man, we as a species might not be sitting here right now. I might not be typing this and it not being read. That's not a stretch in my opinion. It's been said about dogs that it's the "best bargain" man has ever made. I have to agree. Think about what dogs give us and yet they ask for so little in return. They serve us for the merest scraps of our time and love and never expect it back in return. It's also said, and I agree wholeheartedly, that "dogs are the only thing that love you more than they love themselves."

Unlike any other animal on the planet, dogs have been molded by humankind to fit our needs in a variety of ways. From keeping us safe, to assisting those in need, to simple companionship. No animal has the utility that dogs do. Of course, when we get the puppy dog eyes it could be the other way around.

Dogs, at least to me, hold a special place that all too often mankind fails to appreciate and treat with the respect they deserve. To me, that underscores the times that humans also fail to live up to what dogs give us. No animal should be abused or harmed in the manner that is all too often inflicted on dogs. Dogs above all others deserve a special place. They have earned it. Horses? Cats? Pigs? Cattle? Sure, they have their utility in various ways. I'm not trying to dissuade anyone here except to point out there are animals across the spectrum, wild and domesticated, and then there are dogs.

Another important point is I'm not trying to sway anyone from their particular views, whether it be companionship of cats, to animal husbandry. It needs to be said that a person's outlook on the matter is their own.

That brings us finally to Gunner. Gunner came to us towards the later portion of his life. We didn't, and never will, know exactly what went on before we entered the picture in his life. We only have the barest fragments and a lot of speculation as to what may have come before. We had no way of knowing and had a lot to learn and fill in a lot of blanks as we went. Suffice to say that prior to us, a lot of his life was unknown.

Throughout the journey of our time with Gunner, I've talked a lot about how he affected me. When in reality, it wasn't just me. He affected a lot of people simply by his story being told, even before this book. By giving him a voice, he has been able to reach far beyond his realm of my family, and I hope he has touched many people. His story is one of abandonment, through love and loss, and ultimately hope.

Gunner, more so than any other dog I've met or let alone owned, has changed my life. I hope that in reading this, I tell his story in a meaningful way. A story of the most amazing dog and one I fervently hope to see again one day. It's said that every owner will have that one dog that will be the best dog they'll ever have in their life. For me, I've been blessed to not only have one, but two. In that I count myself rich beyond measure.

Enough of that though, here is Gunner's story, in his own words.

MY NAME IS GUNNER

Prior to July 2018

GUNNER THE BEAGLE HERE!

Hi, my name is Gunner. I'm a dog! People say I'm a beagle. I'm not sure what the difference is, but I do know I was born on March 14, 2008. I have no idea what any of those mean as I can't count beyond, one, two, lots! I just know it!

I live outside with another dog called Bandit. Bandit sorta looks like me, but different too. We sometimes huddle together at night to stay warm, and to keep each other company. The summers get really hot and the winters really cold. We have to huddle more when the white stuff comes down from the sky. I don't like being outside when the white stuff falls from the sky. I don't like the white stuff at all. The nights get really long and it seems like it will never get warm again, but eventually it does.

I like it more when it's warmer. I spread out and try to get as warm as I can!

Most of all I'm bored. I see people and want to say hi to them, but I never really get a chance to. My kennel seems to be my whole world.

The world passes me by and sometimes I wonder, is there more than this? I mean I know I'm a good dog. I'm kind and gentle and want to be loved. Bandit and I have each other, but I really want to be in a pack with my own hoomans.

NEW BEGINNINGS
July 2018

🐾 GUNNER THE BEAGLE HERE!

I'm in a strange place, it's cozy here and I have a kennel like my former dwelling, but it's bigger. There are ladies here that are so nice to me. They pet me a lot and talk to me a lot too. I really don't know what to think. People really haven't talked to me that much in my whole life. They seem to like me a lot and tell me I'm a "good boy!" They also say something about "new beginnings and all?"

They say this is a shelter and that sometimes dogs stay here for a while and that this will be my home for a bit. Home? I had a place I used to live, was that a home? Maybe I don't know what a home is?

The nice shelter ladies give me treats and let me wander from time to time, and I get to meet other hoomans and dogs! But they say "I'm older" and they look worried about that. Don't ask me why.

I have my own cot and can go wee-wee outside anytime I want, but at night it gets scary sometimes when the shelter ladies leave. It's warm and there are other dogs here, but it gets really quiet. I and the other dogs get really lonely.

This place is strange though, a lot of the other dogs here seem sad too. Did they do something wrong to end up here like me? I hope not. I can smell that they are upset, sometimes me too. I must have done something wrong like they did because one day I found myself here and I don't know why. Maybe people didn't like me. I didn't do anything wrong.

The other dogs get sad just like me. They seem to be looking for something. They keep looking for hoomans maybe? I don't really know what that means either as I never really had hoomans to really call my own.

SOMETHING WRONG WITH ME?

August 2018

GUNNER THE BEAGLE HERE!

I've been at the shelter for a while now, but how long? I don't know, I'm a dog, my counting is one, two, lots, remember?

I see lots of my doggy friends in the kennels nearby. We bark at each other and keep each other company. At night, sometimes it gets lonely even though I'm used to that. During the day, we get to go outside and run around and play. I can't run around like them, even though I want to. I get tired as I'm older.

BUT NO ONE IS COMING TO SEE ME. IS THERE SOMETHING WRONG WITH ME?

Bandit is here too! Sometimes we go outside and play together, but we don't sleep in the same kennel anymore. Bandit is more shy than me. He seems sad and doesn't understand this place anymore than me. I try to cheer him up when we go outside. He likes that a lot and it makes me happy. Sometimes we search around for food even though we have enough. The shelter ladies say that Bandit is "my partner in crime." I have no idea what a crime is, I just like the only friend I've ever had.

Every once in a while, I see some hoomans come to the shelter and some of my friends nearby are really, really excited, and bark a lot! The shelter ladies get really excited too and tell my doggy friends they are "going home" or say things about "a forever home." But no one is coming to see me. Is there something wrong with me? The shelter ladies are ever so nice, but I hear them whispering about "I don't know if it will happen for him, he's older." Sometimes they are sad and look at me sad and begin to cry.

What does that mean? I don't understand. All I want is a hooman of my own. Do I get a forever home too? I'm a good boy, I promise! I hope someone takes me to a forever home too.

STILL HERE...
September 2018

GUNNER THE BEAGLE HERE!

Still here with the shelter ladies. I still get to sleep all day if I want and go outside whenever I want, but it's not like this "forever home" I keep hearing about! That sounds really great!

Today Bandit left me. I'm sad. He was my only friend until I came here. For many changes of the seasons, it was just the two of us. He's younger than me at least that's what the shelter ladies say. That must be why some of the hoomans came and took him to his "forever home" and not me? I wonder, do older dogs like me get to go to "forever homes" too? I hope so.

I hope Bandit is happy with his new hoomans and he tells them to take me home too! That would be great. He can get to his new home and they tell them "you need to come and get my friend Gunner too. He's lonely at the shelter without me and a good boy!" I am, I am a good boy!

Oh please, please, I hope Bandit's new hoomans listen to him and take me home too!

At least the sun was out and it was warm today, but the air is starting to get chilly at night. Must also mean the white stuff will be falling from the sky and the nights getting really cold and long. Bandit and I had to keep each other company and warm, but it's warm in the shelter so it might not be too bad. I still don't like that white stuff.

I know what to do. I need to get as much of the warmth before it's gone. It's one of the only things that kept me going through the long white stuff season. And now that I don't have Bandit to keep me company, what will I do?

MY FOREVER FAMILY?

10-21-18

 **GUNNER THE BEAGLE HERE!**

I've been at the shelter for a long while and it seems like maybe this place is where I'll live from now on. Nights are lonely although there are other dogs nearby. Some of my other friends have left and other dogs have taken their place. Then they leave too. It seems that the shelter isn't a forever home like they keep saying, but a place where some dogs stay for a short while, but I will always stay?

It's something with the different hoomans who come and visit the nice shelter ladies. They come in, look at the dogs and then "take one of them home." Do I get to do that someday?

I'm not sure when (since I can't tell time) but some nice, new hoomans came to visit me today with some of the shelter ladies.

I sniffed the small hooman a lot, he seemed okay. I really, really liked the other hooman. I liked him most of all, I like his smell! They were the first hoomans who came to visit me and spent a lot of time with me, I like these hoomans. But they left and didn't take me with them?

The shelter ladies are crying slightly? Did I do something that these hoomans did not like? I'm a good boy. The shelter ladies tell me so! All I want is some hoomans to be my family! Hoomans, will you take me home? I'll be good! COME BACK HOOMANS!

GUNNER'S PERSON HERE

On this day we met our new dog for the first time. Even though this is the first time we entered his life, he has been in ours for some time before today. We found him online and had been watching him and his story at the shelter. What brought us to him was my wife seeing a particular photo of Gunner with the biggest smile ever. She was smitten.

It's true: no one else has inquired about him, no one else has come to visit. Other dogs have left the shelter since his arrival, but not him. And that is one of the problems (through no fault of their own) of senior dogs. Ten and a half is on the older side for a dog and tougher to get adopted out. It's likely that because of his age no one else saw what we saw in him and in that we are fortunate. Fortunate because he might not otherwise have become ours.

What Gunner himself also doesn't know is: he's already ours, even before we came to visit him. It's simply a matter of timing that is keeping him at the shelter for the moment. After we talked at length to bring another dog into the house, we went back and forth. We already have a Golden Retriever named Timber. She is good with other dogs so that isn't the issue. It's going from one to two dogs. Nor was the timing working. But in the end, we worked out an agreement with the shelter.

He seems to be most interested in my son, but a bit wary of all of us. Meek and mild would be two ways to describe him. It's readily apparent that he is a gentle soul.

I'm still a bit uncertain of a senior dog and from what we understand, one that lived outside his entire life. But my wife has been drawn to him as if he was meant to be ours. We're his new hoomans. We paid the fees for him and he is now a part of our family; ours now and forever. Even from this brief meeting we know it.

Oh and most importantly, what does he look like? He's a fifteen inch purebred, about 30 lbs, male, and a typical tri-colored beagle: black, brown, and light tan fur with four white socks. There is one main exception. Given his age, he has quite a lot of white on his face and ears.

WHY NOT ME?

12-4-18

GUNNER THE BEAGLE HERE!

I'm bushed today because I was outside running around in the play area. It's fenced in and some of the other dogs go there too. There was some of the white stuff on the ground and I got tired quickly. I can't do the stuff I used to when I was young. I did run around with the other dogs for a while though. After I went wee-wee on the white stuff, I went back inside. It's cold! There is some white stuff coming down from the sky right now.

My friends Jambi and Zephyr are running around like crazy inside! I really want to run around too, but I can't. I guess I'll just supervise them. They are my new friends now that Bandit has left. Sometimes Jambi curls up next to me when we are out of our kennels just like Bandit. I like it when he keeps me company. Sometimes he does what the shelter ladies call a "photo bomb." I have no idea what that means.

Some other dogs have left and people are coming to look at Jambi and Zephyr. But not me. I guess no one wants me. Where are those nice people who came to see me? I don't think they are ever coming back. I don't think they liked or wanted me. Why not me? No one wants me.

I guess this is my new home then. It's bigger than my old one, but in a lot of ways the same. I'm lonely. I miss Bandit. I'm sad too. Why don't people want me?

For years I saw people and wanted to be with them. The nice shelter ladies give me lots of love, but they can't always be here. They say Christmas is coming. Something about putting up a tree inside and presents and being grateful they say? At least I'm not outside, that's something, I guess.

GOING HOME?

12-12-18

GUNNER THE BEAGLE HERE!

I'm still at the shelter, but it's a weird day! I don't know what it is, but the shelter ladies here are so happy and sad at the same time? Some of them are crying and they keep saying "tears of happiness" and "we're so happy for you buddy, it's happening!" They also keep saying I'm "going home?" As in a forever home like my friends here? No way, the other dogs are lucky, they get to go to "forever homes," not me.

But, they keep saying it and looking at me and hugging and petting me? Maybe it really is true? They are standing around laughing, smiling, and eating food? They say it's a party for me? What the heck is a party though?

Never mind that right now, what gives with this "party?" There is lots of food, but none of it is for me? They keep saying it's my party, but it looks like it's for them! Maybe if I'm sneaky, I can grab the goods! Better yet, if I give them "the doggo head tilt" maybe that will work!

Instead they give me the orange crunchy sticks...when no one is looking, I swipe some of the stuff they are eating off the table, I think they keep saying pizza. I have no idea what that is, but it's good. I snatch some "crusts" as they call them before they can stop me!

They go back to saying "going home", but they can't be right. They are all laughing and happy. No, this can't be right, other dogs leave, not me. They are talking to someone on those phone things. The nice shelter lady says "they are on their way now and will be here in a half an hour." All the nice shelter ladies are really happy now!

Is it finally time to have my own hoomans? Really?

GUNNER'S PERSON HERE

The day is finally here. The timing is finally right to get our old pup and take him home. Home. From this day forward, that is what he will have with us, a forever home.

All four of us: my wife, daughter, son, and I take the truck to go get Gunner. The ride there is anxious, that feeling of newness, of the unknown as well. How will Gunner react? How will he fit into our lives? Will he even like us? We've only met him once. Will he even remember us?

From the bits and pieces we have heard from his previous life, we want it to be better. We don't know and can never know all the particulars. All we know is he was dropped off at the shelter, his breed, his age, and what we see. It's going to be a learning experience for all of us, Gunner included, as we learn about him.

Regardless of the thoughts in my head, of the past and the future ahead, we are determined to make his life great.

LEAVING THE SHELTER?

12-12-18

GUNNER THE BEAGLE HERE!

The hoomans who came to visit me...they....they...came back! They are smiling and happy and petting me! The shelter ladies are all crying again, A LOT! Wait, did I do something wrong? Am I going back outside to live, did I not do something right? The white stuff is on the ground, I don't want to go back and live outside. Please, please, please shelter ladies I'll be a good boy! Don't make me go...

Wait...the hoomans... who came to visit me are crowding around me now, hugs and treats? Did they come back for me? Are they my forever family? The really nice shelter lady says so, they are my family! The nice shelter lady is taking something called "photos" on the phone thing. I can't believe this is finally happening!

I remember their smell. I like them, the hooman! I remember him! I really like his smell! Maybe he is the leader of the pack. More tears of happiness from the shelter ladies? I'm so confused. They keep saying leaving? Everyone is so happy! There is the hooman, a lady hooman and two smaller hoomans, a boy and a girl?

The nice shelter lady hands my leash to the hooman and we all go outside. Are we are leaving the shelter? The shelter ladies are waving as we walk out? I'm leaving!

We are going outside to a truck? I love trucks! I love to ride in them! The white stuff on the ground is sticking to my paws and it's cold. I don't like this stuff, but I don't care right now. I have a forever family! I love trucks and rides in them! The hooman picks me up, ("oof") and into the back with the smaller hoomans? They are petting me non-stop and happy. I'm leaving the shelter! Where are we going?

Doesn't matter, I'm smiling.

GUNNER'S PERSON HERE

Today, Gunner truly became ours. No, that is not right, he was always ours, we just didn't have him from the beginning. No matter what, be it good or bad, whether it's a short time or a long one, Gunner will be with us forever, and he will never have to worry about affection, shelter, food, warmth, and water ever again. Safe to say we love him from the start.

We're bringing him home a few weeks before Christmas. Add to this having just got back from vacation and it's a perfect ending to the year, and a great present for the entire family. Not sure our Golden Retriever is going to look at it that way, but she has a companion now too.

And indeed, on the way home, my wife takes a great photo as the kids pet him. He has the biggest smile on his face as if he knew he was going home and any small doubts we had that we are doing the right thing simply vanished.

FOREVER HOME

12-12-18

GUNNER THE BEAGLE HERE!

What is this new place? I'm happy to leave the shelter. The shelter ladies were ever so nice, but is this home. What is going on here? This is a really big house, although I am a small dog...I want to go inside! There is another dog here too, a shaggy golden one? Not sure what to think of her. This place is mine, I'll show her! She sniffs me and I her, looks like she is fine.

This is my forever home? I still can't believe I finally have my forever family! This can't be happening. Is this what the shelter ladies were crying over? Oh boy!

It's warm in here and smells like food! Woah this place is big. Lots of places to go wander to. Where is the food? The hoomans are also saying something about "these blankets are yours!" What is a blanket? (sniffs). Well, it's not food, it's soft though, I'm supposed to lay on something soft? I can't remember if I had any of these before.

Wait food too? I have my own bowl over there? And my own bed? This place is great! What the heck is with a tree inside a house, and it has lights on it? Am I supposed to go wee-wee on that?

More stuff to explore! (sniffs). Woah there is hot air coming out of that hole in the ground? Maybe I'll curl up near it. Ahhh very warm and cozy.

GUNNER'S PERSON HERE

As I lifted him out of the truck, he pads right to the door. It's as if he knows where to go already and eagerly heads in. Once inside, he meets our Golden, Timber. She is good with other dogs and no issues arise with Gunner. She pads over to him with her tail wagging slightly and begins to sniff him. For his part Gunner sniffs Timber back but for a mere second and is off exploring. It's clear he is interested in his new surroundings more than her.

He wanders around, sniffs and looks at us. He explores some more and seems to like it. Quickly he realizes that the kitchen is the focal point and where all the food is. He finds his water bowl (and Timber's) and his bed and promptly lays down by the hot air register. It doesn't matter. He is home and I think (and hope) he feels it. Probably not though, I know it will take him a while to feel safe and part of the family. That whole three days, three weeks, three months for a shelter dog to decompress, and fit in and feel secure.

Gunner watches us cook and is quick to see if there is anything for him. It's apparent that he is very food driven. Sure beagles are that, but he is intent on it. For his age, he is spry and snacks quickly upon any food "dropped" on the floor. Timber gets in on the action too.

I'm struck by the thought that there is so much we don't know about him. We're all going to have to find it out together. I also wonder just how bewildering is all of this to him? As in does he not have any idea what any of this means?

Welcome home Gunner...welcome home.

I LIKE MY CAVE

12-14-18

GUNNER THE BEAGLE HERE!

This place seems to be nice, same with the hoomans. I wish they would give me as many treats as the nice shelter ladies! They were giving me lots! The hooman says something about me being "portly?" The lady hooman says that's not very nice! I'm not sure what they are talking about. Maybe it's supposed to be funny?

There is still the white stuff outside, but I only have to see it when I go outside to go wee-wee! It's lightly falling from the sky. I can remember lots of times like this. It meant it was going to be very cold soon.

There is no kennel out there in the back yard. Does this mean I'm staying inside all the time? I get to live inside in a home with the hoomans! It's the best! I mean I've been inside for a little while, but I thought I'd have to go outside eventually...

There is a cave filled with the soft blankets that the hoomans say is for me. It's cozy in there and sometimes I like to go lay down inside and look out of it. They say it's a "crate?" I have no idea what that is. It reminds me of the shelter. I hope my friends at the shelter are finding homes too.

I wonder why the golden dog doesn't go in there? She just flops down wherever. Sometimes I try to lay down next to her and get warm, sometimes she lets me. I guess she never had to huddle together with a friend outside? She must be lucky. Other times she gets up and moves. Oh well. I guess I'll just go back to my cave.

GUNNER'S PERSON HERE

Since he came home, he's been inside with us and it's clear he's not sure what to make of it.

The cave as he calls it, is Gunner's crate. When Timber was much younger she used it, but now that she is older she doesn't. We lined it with blankets and made it comfortable for him. We're not sure what exactly he will like and dislike and we have no idea if he even had soft things. He sniffs the blankets and goes inside, does the dog circles and lays down. We don't close it and let him be. It's likely all of this is a bit overwhelming and we want him to feel safe.

We continue to leave it open for him and in the first few days of being home, he sometimes goes in and sits looking out. He doesn't seem to mind it and seems comforted by it to some degree. Perhaps it's some of that primal wolf instinct of safety equaling being in a cave or den. Perhaps it's some of his former life, or maybe even something of the shelter that makes him feel safe. He doesn't stay in there continuously, but he's observing. I have a feeling he doesn't know what to make of it all.

Everything is fine buddy, you're safe now. Even if you don't know it or feel it yet, you are loved. And you always will be. I promise.

-2019-
GROOMING, WHAT THE HECK IS THAT?

1-5-19

GUNNER THE BEAGLE HERE!

What is going on around here? The shaggy golden dog? She went on a truck ride with my hooman! I'm not happy about that as they were gone a long while! I like riding in trucks!

Not happy, where are they? There is a lot of white stuff out there. I don't want to have to search for them in this. Maybe the lady hooman knows? Nope, she's of no help. The small hooman? He's sleeping? Really?

Eventually they come back and she looks different? Not only does she look different. But she smells funny too! She was all shaggy before and now she is not. The lady hooman says something about "what a pretty girl you are." She also says she "smells great". Ugh, I don't want to smell like that, I like my smell! Something about grooming?

Pretty? Huh? The hooman is looking at me weird and saying something about "It's bath time Gunner." No way? I don't like those things. Time to go and hide! I don't want to get wet!

You can't make me! You can't pick me up ("oof") and take me to the tub! Darn it, couldn't get away. Let's. Get. This. Over. With.

GUNNER'S PERSON HERE

Timber likes or at least tolerates going to the groomer. Shaggy dog in, perfectly groomed girl out. Timber especially likes the rides in the summer where she can do the dog thing and stick her head out the window. Winter rides she likes to curl up on the seat. The issue is as a puppy she was never introduced to a brush and it's a fight to brush her properly between visits.

Gunner watched us leave and seemed a bit upset that he wasn't the one to go on the truck ride.

Gunner? Yeah...let's just say his first bath was an experience. From what we understand he was an outdoor dog his whole life. Naturally he associates water with cold I imagine. He tolerates it but only barely. Plus bathing a beagle in January inside the house? Yeah...he did about as best as we could have hoped for. He tolerated it but you could tell it was not a favorite thing with him.

The bathroom becomes an extreme hazard as he tries to get out of the tub. Water goes flying and it's a rush to try and dry him as we can't take him outside due to the temperature.

Nails were a fight too and I was mindful not to stress him too much. He's been good adjusting to our life and routine, but it hasn't quite even been a month. In the future, it's to the Vet for the nails as they are just down the road.

A lot of this early stage is learning as we go with Gunner. There is no way to predict just how he will react and we have no basis to understand if he has had a positive or negative experience with something. All we can do is be patient.

BEEPING!

GUNNER THE BEAGLE HERE!

SO SCARED, SO SCARED...WHAT IS THAT NOISE?

I just wanna go and hide, Timber is not worried, why isn't she? The lady hooman was in the kitchen cooking something when suddenly it got really smoky and this really loud beeping started and it's scary! I've never heard anything like this before.

My hooman is scurrying around trying to make it stop. Hurry up hooman! It could be dangerous! I need to hide, maybe I can hide on the couch! The smaller hooman is there and I'm shaking, he says it will be okay, but I've never heard something like this.

I'M SHAKING ALL OVER! MAKE THAT SOUND GO AWAY HOOMAN!

GUNNER'S PERSON HERE

Adventures in the kitchen caused the smoke detector to trigger. I'll also add, this happens on occasion as our oven can run very hot at times.

We didn't think twice about it as Timber has heard it before and barely even opens an eye from her bed. Gunner on the other hand? He was terrified by it. He ran and hopped up on the couch shaking where my son found him and started petting him to calm him down. We never really thought about the fact that for him, a lot of things are brand new and this is likely the first time he ever heard the noise and not knowing what it was. Add to it how loud these alarms are and it's easy to see why he was scared.

This, like a lot of other things, was brand new for us too. Our previous Golden, Teddy, was scared of everything; loud noises, thunder, fireworks, you name it. Timber? Not so much.

It also got me wondering just how much is new to him. How much did he miss as a puppy? From what we understand he lived in a kennel. He has no interest in toys. Walks? Brand new to him? The one thing I am certain is he likes truck rides and if he sees one he always wants to get into it.

In all, it puts Gunner's short time with us so far into a different perspective. For him, a lot of stuff is truly new. Things we might take for granted, unlike Timber, who has lived inside her whole life is unfazed by this. And in a way, in the time we've had Gunner, perhaps will be one of the best things is him experiencing things to us that are ordinary or mundane, but unknown to him. Seeing these everyday things through a fresh set of eyes, one's that are as pure as can be. I can't state this enough, Gunner doesn't have a mean bone in his body.

PINING FOR MY PERSON

3-3-19

GUNNER THE BEAGLE HERE!

What the heck is it with my hooman? He leaves in the sun up time and then comes home later? He does this most days and I have to go in my crate! I don't want to go in my crate...ZZZ. Then the other hooman comes home first and she lets me out of jail! Hey wait a minute how come Timber doesn't have to go in the crate? Just me? Anyways I got to go outside and go wee-wee.

Where is my hooman? He is not here! Maybe if I go to the

front door and stare intently out he'll appear! HE'S NOT HERE! I'M UPSET! I guess I'll just go and lay in Timber's bed, "move out of there Timber!"

This isn't working. I guess I'll go and lay next to the chair of the other hooman. She's okay I guess. I'M PINING FOR MY HOOMAN!

HE'S STILL NOT HOME!   I'm crying now...

WAIT!   I HEAR HIS TRUCK! HE'S HOME!   I'M GOING TO THE OTHER DOOR!   HE'S HOME!   I MUST GO GREET HIM AT THE DOOR!

GUNNER'S PERSON HERE

We have talked about how he gets so eager when it's close to the time for me to get home. My wife gets home several hours before me and she gets to watch the ritual that is Gunner waiting for my arrival (the kids get home before me too).

We experiment with different times and somehow he always knows when I will be home. Yet somehow, almost always to the minute, he would start getting upset and start pacing twenty five minutes before I arrived.

Other times I would concentrate and tell him I'm coming home (mentally) and sure enough, my wife would report that he would start getting antsy. Weird, but true.

The odd part is when my wife would come home he wouldn't even stir in his crate. Loud noises? Nope. He wouldn't move anything short of her opening up the crate. And even then he might not move at all. Sometimes, as strange as this may sound, even opening the crate he still wouldn't stir!

In a way I'm a bit jealous. My wife gets to experience this. She gets to observe day after day what Gunner goes through and sees what he does, but it's something that I never can. But truth be told it's something I'm fine with. It's a small thing that is big when one considers it. It's a part of Gunner being with us. Yes it's about me, but something that will always be through her eyes. I'm completely fine with that.

The flip side of this is she is the one who found Gunner in the hopes he would "be her dog." Let's just say Gunner has his own mind about that.

COUCH, SHH DON'T TELL

4-28-19

GUNNER THE BEAGLE HERE!

I've been with these hoomans for a while now, they seem nice. I understand why the shelter ladies were so happy for me to find my forever home, it sure seems like it.

Timber has gotten used to being bossed around. I try to be nice. She's my only dog friend here, just like Bandit before. But when it comes to who is in charge, it's me! I get the treats first...Timber you've had them all your life! Dinner time same thing, me first!

The one strange thing is why I can't sleep on those couch things the hoomans sit on? My hooman says no, "no dogs on the couch." What the heck is that? Why not?

Sometimes when the lady hooman and the smaller hoomans are home, they let me on it though! Even when he is home the smaller hoomans try and sneak me up when my hooman isn't looking. I'm quiet and stealthy! Then take photos of me on those phone things and say "how cute." I think it means that they like me!

But then every once in a while my hooman says I'm not supposed to be up here, maybe if I stay quiet he won't see me! Shhh!

GUNNER'S PERSON HERE

Yeah...no dogs on the couch. That has been a rule for quite some time, although I'll freely admit we haven't always been consistent with it over the years. Gunner is persistent (of course he's a beagle) and he keeps trying to worm his way up there. Doesn't help that the rest of the pack in the house is egging him on. Of course Timber is perplexed why she can't get up there too.

It's likely that he likes the couch as he picks the spot where I sit. Naturally this spot smells like me and he seems to be gravitating more and more to me.

So of course, I have to be the bad guy and shoo him off. As I head to the kitchen, he follows me and then follows me back. My wife noticed as soon as I left, he perked up and starting watching where I was going.

I shoo him off again. Showing that I'm not entirely heartless, I actually lay down on the floor with him and he parks himself between my lower legs on a blanket I put out for him. That seems to do the trick because once he settles in he puts his snout on my legs and drifts off to sleep.

Memories bring me back to our previous house where I used to do this for Teddy, our first Golden Retriever. We would watch TV and I'd lay on the floor and he'd "beach" himself on me as we called it. I'd continue to pet him as we watched and he would have me do this for hours if he could. It's good to do this again, but with Gunner it's slightly different. With Gunner he just wants to be near me or in contact with me, but not necessarily pet. Perhaps it's reassuring that I'm not going to leave him? Don't worry buddy, you're not going anywhere.

BELLY, ARE YOU NUTS?

5-28-19

GUNNER THE BEAGLE HERE!

Its been good here with the hoomans! My hooman seems to be around more on these things called "weekends?" What the heck is a weekend? All I know he is here more so I can keep an eye on him and he can't sneak way. I'm wise to you hooman!

Anyways, the hooman was petting me which I'm starting to like and I decided to flop over and let him rub my belly! That felt good! He even scratched the base of my tail! I can't get to that place, it felt so good too! I think I'll keep my hooman! Scratch my tail again!

Then he scratched my chest for me too. What gives hooman? You know all the places I can't reach and itch! Must be those hand things the hoomans have, I just have paws.

You got treats too?

Alright, I've had enough for now, time to go nap!

GUNNER'S PERSON HERE

Gunner has been very tentative about touch. Timber? One could pet for hours and she would want it to be continued. Gunner, on the other hand, seems almost ambivalent about being pet. It's possible he never had a lot of physical contact? With no way to know for sure, we are being patient with him and proceeding on his terms. It's not that he flinches or recoils from it, rather it seems as if he just doesn't know what to make of it.

Then out of the blue while petting him he rolled over and

showed his belly. I grinned as I knew we had turned a corner.

After many months, he finally felt safe enough to do this. Sometimes it's the simple things in life and this is one of them. I will always have that image in my mind as he gently rolled over and let me pet him on his stomach, that he felt safe enough to do so.

As suddenly as it started Gunner had enough. Most of the dogs we have had would stay there for hours if it meant belly rubs. Gunner seems to have had his fill and is done. It's a good start in terms of trust between he and I and at this point I think he feels that he is part of the pack.

He pads off a bit, does the dog circles and lays down out of arms reach from me. Every once in a while he will open an eye. There seems to be this part of him that keeps a wary eye on us. Not that I think he's worried about something bad happening, rather I think he keeps an eye out so that he knows that we are still there. It's as if he is worried we won't be there when he wakes up. Again buddy no need to worry, I'm here, you're safe.

RETURNED?

6-3-19

GUNNER THE BEAGLE HERE!

What is going on here? The hoomans have dropped Timber and I off at some place that looks like shelter? Is this a shelter? Did we do something wrong? Was I not good? Please, please don't make me leave home. I'll be good. I don't want to stay here! Don't want to be returned!

Wait my hooman is driving away! Come back hooman! No don't leave me here! I'm a good boy!

Timber is here with me too? Did she do something wrong too? She doesn't seem too upset? What is wrong with her? I don't understand.

Looks like we have a new home with the two of us inside this cage? There are some other dogs here too and it seems like the shelter. They look anxious just like me. I only see one lady and she doesn't look like the nice shelter lady?

I want to go back home!

GUNNER'S PERSON HERE

I'm not going to lie, this was hard. We haven't had him that long and I was concerned what his behavior would be.

The demands of travel soccer means sometimes we're at out-of-town tournaments and that means kenneling the dogs. Usually we have someone house/dog sit, but this time, we can't get anyone.

It was tough. I wondered what was going through his mind.

Timber has been through this before and is easy going. Plus she has been with us for years. Gunner on the other hand? We have only had him for around six months. Granted they can't count like we can, but did he feel he was being abandoned again? Did he feel like he was going back to the shelter? That thought of stressing him is likewise distressing to me. I really don't want him to think he's being abandoned again.

It seemed like it was forever, but in reality it was just a weekend. We took Monday off too and arrived at the dog boarding nearly an hour before it opens. We're not supposed to be here this early, a fact that I "forgot." It's amazing to think that, in just this amount of time, even being apart from Gunner for two days is two days too long. Amazing also that in six months he's become that ingrained in our lives.

Once he saw me, he was as happy as could be and was practically pulling me towards the truck. We load Timber in the back as the kids are in school and of course Gunner has to be in front. This time he is beached on my wife's lap who is loving every minute of it. She pets him nonstop and he is "happy panting" and smiles the whole way home. You can tell he is relieved. Timber just curls up in the backseat as if it was no big deal.

The smile on his face as we drive home is something that was pure happiness to behold. At the same time, I hope we don't have to kennel them again.

FENCE THING IS UP!

7-4-19

GUNNER THE BEAGLE HERE!

My hooman has been outside for a lot of months now working: digging holes (I help with that!), chasing off rabbits (I really help with that!), and doing stuff. Most nights he's out there doing work and comes inside very tired, sweaty, and sore. Timber and I cheer him up and clean him up sniffing him. He usually smells good to us too! We like how he smells when he comes inside! Although the lady hooman says "you stink, take a shower!" Hah, you have to go take a bath I think, but not me!

He looks to be putting up a really big fence, just like I had at the shelter with the other dogs. Timber doesn't know what to make of this.

Today my hooman said "it's ready." He let us both out at the same time and we got to run around. Timber wanders around for a bit...but the fence goes all the way around. She looked really confused. I started sniffing the fence line. I'll make my escape soon! In the meantime, I need to go wee-wee.

GUNNER'S PERSON HERE

After a lot of hard work, the fence is up. One of my biggest concerns back in December when we got Gunner was two dogs we would have to let outside on leads with no fenced in yard. The only way we found for this to work was one at a time. I started in April and got it all up in roughly three months. What Gunner notes is true, lots of work, drilling, digging, and setting the fence, gates, etc. His "help?" Sure... I guess. In all seriousness, there were times when he just wanted to make sure he could see where I was.

In the end it's worth it. We have a fairly big back yard and the dogs can roam freely. Gunner especially likes to sit outside and sun himself. I have to wonder if this is so ingrained in him from living outdoors for so long; that he sunned himself after the long winters here.

I'm also saddened by the thought of just how much space he may have had prior. From what we understand he and Bandit lived outside in a kennel. As for how long? He was about ten and a half when we got him...I hope it wasn't his entire life. How big was it? Likewise an unknown. In any event, the dogs, or at least Timber, are nonplussed. We let them out, they do their business and they want to head back in.

HELPING MY PERSON OUT!

8-29-19

GUNNER THE BEAGLE HERE!

No sooner did my hooman finish the fence thing to keep us in, he started with something that looks like a big doghouse? I hope it's not for me. It looks nice though...wait what am I saying, I don't want to live outside again! Don't put a kennel on the side of it either, I don't want to go in there!

He's doing it himself? I'm a super helpful beagle! I'll help hooman! Let me, well...okay...I think I'll just lay down on the decking and watch? Does that count as helping? Scratch my belly too while you're at it! Better yet, I think I'm going to just lay here soaking up the sun.

He works a lot of time on it. How long I don't know, I'm a dog, remember? But eventually, he puts it all together, paints it, and makes a sign. He tells the lady hooman its like one his grandfather had and it says "Dad's Dog House" on it. Hah hooman, it's yours. You made your own kennel, now you have to sleep outside while I go inside to sleep!

Wait that means I won't be sleeping near you! You better think this over. I want to sleep inside, so do you!

GUNNER'S PERSON HERE

Gunner has nothing to worry about, he's never living outside ever again. For that matter, I'm not sleeping outside either unless I'm camping. During the construction of the fence, he couldn't come outside for obvious reasons. During the construction of the shed however, he wants to be near and observe what is going on.

In terms of him "helping?" Let's just say he engaged in more of a supervisory role. The most he did was lay around on the deck watching, lay in the shade near the shovels, and a few times under the wheel barrow. Doesn't matter one bit. This was the first time he was really, really attached to me in the sense of wherever I went, he had to go too. We've taken to calling him my barnacle because he's attached to me now. Over the last months especially he has bonded to the family, but today was the first time he really looked at me and I him where we both "got it."

If I moved around and he couldn't see me, he got frantic and would have to seek me out. If I was on the other side of the shed putting up a wall, he had to move so I would be in his line of sight.

It's a really strange feeling for me however. I've had dogs before, but I've never had one imprint on me so strongly. Our first Golden, Teddy was sort of like this but I was more first among equals as he loved everyone. Not so with Gunner. The other odd part of this is Gunner's age. He's eleven now and I would think this is behavior a puppy would engage in. Doesn't matter though, I wouldn't want it any other way. From this day forward, I'm his hooman and he is my dog.

FOOTBALL SEASON
9-8-19

GUNNER THE BEAGLE HERE!

The nights are getting a bit longer here and the air is changing, I can smell it with my sniffer! My hoomans have been taking me for more walks. My hooman says something about "the leaves changing soon." I like this time of year with the different colors of leaves. It gives me something different to go wee-wee on!

Something else the hooman says, "It's football season!" Don't ask me what that means, all I know is he watches something called a "Tee Vee" and says stuff to the lady hooman. Sometimes he's happy (rarely), more often than not he's disappointed saying "Well of course my team didn't win." Then she says, "Yeah well my team is even worse, they really, really, never win!" I have no idea what they mean by winning. I'm winning by being here! Silly hoomans!

Doesn't matter. Timber is sleeping and my hooman beckons me over. He says "Here's some Scotch buddy." I'm not sure what that is, but I lick it off his finger. It's good! Life is good too!

GUNNER'S PERSON HERE

Let me get this out of the way: he's not chugging alcohol here. And yes, I know dogs aren't supposed to have it. However, while watching football, he was staring at me and I gave him some. He liked it, looked at me and then went and laid down.

Not sure why I did it. I've never let any of my other dogs try it, but it figures my "lived his life outdoors beagle" has expensive taste in Scotch.

More so than the Scotch, Gunner (and Timber) like football Sundays for the food, the smells and in the case of Gunner, the companionship. Everyone is home. It's cozy and he's content. The pack as it were is all gathered upstairs and he is happy to be part of it.

In fact looking over, he's in his bed, on his back with his paws slightly twitching as he dreams. He happily whimpers as he dozes and breathes rhythmically. I hope his dreams are good ones. He's content and I imagine he's chasing (and catching) those rabbits he sees in the yard from time to time. All this while I experience never ending frustration rooting for my football team, win some, lose some. At least I have Gunner and that is a win no matter what.

EYE SCARE

9-20-19

🐾 GUNNER THE BEAGLE HERE!

My hooman took me for a ride in the truck today! I love truck rides. And riding with my hooman is best of all!

He lifted me up into the truck ("oof") and I had to go greet him on his side. He likes it when I do that. He seemed very serious though. I could tell he wasn't mad at me as he kept petting me and said "I'm sure it will be alright buddy." Of course it will be alright (no idea what he means), I have you! Silly hooman!

We drive for a bit and he tells me we are going to a clinic. He gets me out and I have to go wee-wee after the long ride. It looks like the shelter. I don't want to go in there! Eventually he says something about a doctor and eye...Oh yeah that lump thing.

He looks really concerned.

Inside it looks familiar, maybe I've been here before? It looks really familiar I'm going crazy, what's behind all those doors!

I meet the doctor, he looks like a Vet to me, but is nice. I can smell his dogs too. He looks at my eye and talks to my hooman. They look at it some more and my hooman smiles and looks very relieved. I like it when my hooman does that. I wonder what he was so upset about? I could smell the worry on him.

GUNNER'S PERSON HERE

Gunner had a non-cancerous lump on his eyelid it turns out. I could not be more relieved than I am right now.

The whole thing scared us. We haven't even had him for a year and the thought of us losing him so soon hit home. We knew adopting a senior dog comes with risks but weren't prepared for something so suddenly.

We went into this with what we thought was a good mindset, but it's incredible to think that in such a short time he has become such an important part of our family.

Apparently with older dogs, some of them can develop these types of things. In the months that we have had him, we have seen a few "tags" develop near his eye only to fall off. This one, however, was larger and more worrisome. Turns out it was nothing too complex and was taken care of very easily.

The odd part of his behavior that I didn't figure out was he was really anxious at the clinic but not for the reason why. He did the same thing at our Vet a while back too then it clicked: he thought he was back at the shelter and was trying to go greet the shelter ladies. Imagine his surprise when he couldn't find them.

In any event, this was tough. Immediately the first thing that jumps into ones head is the dreaded word: cancer. Turns out that wasn't it. I never want to have to worry about his eye, a tumor or cancer ever again. Once was enough!

HALLOWEEN, AKA LOTS OF PEOPLE AT THE DOOR...

10-31-19

GUNNER THE BEAGLE HERE!

It's been raining like crazy all day today. Timber and I hardly want to go outside and "do our business." I have no idea why the silly hoomans call it that. Anyways my hooman has been outside putting up what the other hooman calls "decorations." There is this big, puffy guy in the winds out there too.

It's cold too. The weather and the leaves have changed and I don't like it when that happens. It means the time for the white stuff is coming up.

It gets dark quickly now too, and that's another thing I didn't like. Bandit and I would be cold and it was dark and scary out too. I hope Bandit is inside! I miss Bandit. I hope he is happy.

Anyways there are lots of little hoomans (and some bigger ones) coming to the door and my hoomans are giving them treats! I love treats but they say I can't have these? What gives? You said treats hoomans! I want some! They say "trick or treat" and you give them treats? This is so confusing. Timber is of no help here.

GUNNER'S PERSON HERE

Gunner was quite intrigued by Halloween. Not only was it the repeated perking up to the word "treat" in "Trick or Treat" at the door, but the comings and goings. He was genuinely interested in what was going on. I suspect he just wanted to see all the people.

Throughout the night he was never far from the door, even Timber would sometimes stir or make her way to the door too. Neither was trying to escape, just interested. Then it hit me. I thought about just how strong a dog's sense of smell is and it got me wondering. It could be that dogs have no real interest in what is going on at the door and (paradoxically) "treat" doesn't mean what it normally means, at least for tonight to them. What could very well matter is the smell of all the various people coming and going at the door. Their sense of smell is millions of times stronger than ours and I'm willing to bet this is like going on a walk for them, but in reverse. The smells are being brought to them.

In another way, they are also meeting other dogs. Any dog owner has residual smells of their dog on them that we don't detect, but dogs do. In our neighborhood, there are a tons of dogs and Gunner, while perplexed, seems to be enjoying it and sure enough sniffing at the door. Go to another person's house and they have a dog? What does the dog do? He starts sniffing, smelling your dog, simple really.

I could be completely wrong here, but based on his actions, I think this is exactly what is going on.

NESTING AND SUCH

11-3-19

GUNNER THE BEAGLE HERE!

The nice hoomans have provided me with my own bed (sometimes I kick Timber out of hers) but it's not the way I want it.

The nice lady hooman said something about "it smells like dog" the other day. Well duh lady, I'm a dog! Anyways, she brought it back and it doesn't smell like me anymore. It smells really weird! It smells like flowers, but it is really warm when she puts it down... but no it's not right! Doesn't matter. It's warm...wait what was I saying I'm mad at you lady hooman for making it smell better you say?

On top of that, it's folded? What the heck lady? Maybe I'll go wee-wee on it when she's not looking...it's too neat. Time for me to mess it up! I need to make my nest!

GUNNER'S PERSON HERE

Gunner has settled well into the routine of our lives and the comings and goings of work, school, and whatnot. He has learned that in the Fall, Saturday and Sunday means football which in turn means we're all together and he wants to be with the family. Why not, he is family.

He is however particular about his bed and the way the blankets are and I was FINALLY able to get it on video. The process is fascinating to watch. Of course Gunner has to do the traditional "wolf circles" before he lays down, but more importantly he has to arrange everything just right.

But what to do when you don't have hands? Never fear, he has become an expert with his snout and flipping the blankets up a bit and moving them to his liking. We watch the video time and again and it's the best thing ever. It's great. He just puts his snout underneath the ones he wants to move and just lifts up, rearranging as he goes. They sort of pop up and he deftly flicks them. In the end, he is so very pleased with himself, as if to say "Now this is the way I want it!"

We can't envision just what we did before him. Timber? When it comes to sleeping, she just conks out wherever she wants, no adjusting the bed. But Gunner? He really likes football weekends and when the heat kicks on, he's even happier as his bed is right by a vent.

The shelter says he "landed on all four paws" finding us. No. They are wrong. We did. We didn't know how empty our home was without him. Now with two dogs? Life is great.

CONTENT AS CAN BE

12-8-19

GUNNER THE BEAGLE HERE!

Looks like a whole season has passed. I can tell as the white stuff is starting to fall from the sky again in small amounts, means lots more later. I'm smart like that!

They brought a tree from outside and placed it inside? Am I supposed to go wee-wee on this? They are putting lights and stuff on it. They keep saying something about "Christmas?" I have no idea what that is. Oh wait...I do. A while back they did the same thing. I think it was when I came to live with my hoomans. Yes, I do remember! It seems like a long, long time ago. I can't count remember? Lets see, one, two…a lot of days! The white stuff falls from the sky, my paws get wet, and the tree goes up! I remember that! I get more treats for being a smart dog?

The best part? I'm inside with my hoomans and they feed me all the time and I'm not outside! (Not as much as I really want!) I'm now lucky I'm not out there. I hope no other dogs have to live out there… I remember what that was like and I hope they are all inside and warm like I am now!

GUNNER'S PERSON HERE

One year has come and gone, and in some ways it seems to have flown by. Gunner is warm, happy, and content, as are we. We can't imagine a time before him. It seems like he has always been here. He and Timber get along well, sometimes they both sleep in Timber's bed. I have a feeling for Gunner it's that instinct to cozy up to Bandit that is coming through when he does. Timber doesn't seem to get it though and will move which sometimes leaves Gunner puzzled. Old habits die hard.

Either way Christmas is right around the corner and in a few days it will be one year since we brought him home. An entire year with him. In some ways it was the blink of an eye. So much happened in the past year from the travails of travel soccer, to scouts, to the general hustle and bustle of our lives. And now with Christmas here taking a moment to take stock and realize how truly fortunate we are. Fortunate, most of all, to have two dogs who, while older, are happy and healthy.

As one becomes older, Christmas takes on a different meaning. It's not what you get, but what you have. Cliche? Sure, but at the same time, true. More so with a dog that is a senior. We know we won't have a decade with him so we have to make every year count. Gunner deserves it. Timber is also aging and slowing down and the two have figured it out. That is to say that Gunner is the top dog and Timber defers to him. Christmas is no different and she waits patiently for him to get his treats first.

Even with all of our happiness and joy Gunner has brought us, we are now are mindful of just how many other dogs out there that might be in the same situation he was in not too long ago. We continue to donate to his shelter even after we adopted him, not for any reason of patting ourselves on the back, but to continue to help them in light of having given us such a wonderful gift that is Gunner.

We hope all his shelter friends have found homes and are living their dreams as well or will so shortly, this holiday season.

DREAMING HAPPY DREAMS

GUNNER THE BEAGLE HERE!

Sooo sleepy here...ZZZ, sleeping on my back...tongue hanging out the side. ZZZ...someone is saying something about how I look like some other dog, red doghouse...ZZZ, "the most famous beagle of all," hey...that's me...ZZZ...

(I'm really out of it now, dreaming of chasing...something...ZZZ)

Something about "football", I think I'm drooling out the side of my face...ZZZ...

Now something about "cute noises?" Keep it down silly hoomans... game is loud enough...ZZZ...

GUNNER'S PERSON HERE

Today while we were watching football, he was dreaming and whimpering like we have never heard him before. It was those kind of sounds that every dog owner has heard where you could tell they were good dreams. You can just as easily know when they are having bad ones, this was the opposite.

It's been a bit over a year since he came home and we've watched him and recorded a lot of video of him with all four paws up and sleeping, but today, you could tell he was truly content. He was so peaceful, his breathing rhythmic, and look of just pure joy.

That very famous beagle sleeping on his doghouse in the cartoons? With Gunner's (now) very white face and the coloration of his ears? He looks just like him. Of course Gunner doesn't have to sleep outside though.

Every once and a while he would stir, move in his bed, go check on Timber and usually go back to sleep. Crumple of bags for food while watching football? He might open one eye and look for a handout, but on this day, he was as the wife says, "he's a sleepy potato." Don't look at me, I have no idea why potatoes would be sleepy.

Timber, on the other hand, is more keen to grab snacks when offered. She is also an expert at swiping napkins off my wife's chair. One would think with how long Timber has been doing it that my wife would catch on. I also wonder if she is doing it on purpose as some sort of game. Timber also likes dirty tissues, yuck.

Gunner wants no part of these shenanigans.

There you have a picture of a typical football Sunday at our house in early January. Snow is on the ground. We're warm and watching our favorite sport and we have two great dogs. Life is good. Now if only my football team wasn't so maddening.

I MAKE FUNNY NOISES?

2-22-20

GUNNER THE BEAGLE HERE!

I don't get what is so funny? All of the hoomans are laughing and pointing at me? They better not be making fun of me! I'm just being myself, don't you all say you like that?

I'm sleepy too and keep yawning and then they laugh some more! What gives around here! I just want to go to sleep. Hey

Timber! Go distract them. Not happy with my hooman either.
I think I'll turn my shoulder to him, that will show him! Who am
I kidding, I can't stay mad at my hooman, well, at least for long!
Maybe if pretend to be mad at him he'll understand?

He's saying something about sounding like a cat? What
the heck silly hooman, you always know stuff. I'm a beagle
remember? Duh!

What, even Timber is laughing now too? I thought you were
on my side! Maybe she is getting back at me when I get all the
treats first?

Oh well, I'm going back to sleep, but need to yawn first. WHAT
THE HECK??? They are all laughing again! All I did was yawn. That's
it, I'm going to my cave, that will show them!

GUNNER'S PERSON HERE

I'll say this right off the bat, some of the animal noises
he makes? We wonder if he grew up on a farm because it's
uncanny. His best one is when he yawns: it sounds just like a cat
meowing. If you catch him at the right time and yawn? He does
the mammalian sympathetic yawn right back, in his gunner-
cat sounding yawn! My wife was the first one to notice this and
started calling him Gunner-cat when he does it.

Other times the best ones are when he does the stretch out
and then yawns. I have a feeling that is one of the signs of Gunner
showing true contentment. He'll be in his bed, get up and circle
then stretch out, yawn and go right back to sleep.

Other ones are his snuffly sounds, like a small elephant and
then loud sneezes.

We've had him for a while now and are still learning a lot of
things about him. The weird part is he didn't start making these
noises until now.

Lastly, he lets me know when it's time to go to bed. Around 11:30 at night he'll get up and turn and look at me. Usually we are in the man cave and as I carry him up the stairs, if I yawn on purpose, he'll do it right back. But when he does this and I carry him up, I'm struck with the thoughts of how I always wanted to take care of our previous Golden, Teddy like this. When he was old and after all he had done for us, I'd be able to take care of him in his senior years. Teddy was a great dog. It wasn't meant to be with us as cancer robbed him from us after a bit over 8 years.

With Gunner, I'm able to do this and in someways it makes up for the loss of Teddy. I hope Gunner avoids Teddy's fate and is with us for many years to come.

FRANTIC FOR MY PERSON!

3-7-20

 GUNNER THE BEAGLE HERE!

WHAT IS GOING ON! WHERE IS MY HOOMAN!?!

I SEARCHED THE ENTIRE HOUSE AND HE IS NOT HERE! TIMBER DO YOU KNOW WHERE HE IS? (She is of course no help.)

My hooman should have been here when I woke up, but he's not. Wait a minute, I remember now he said something about "camping?" What the heck is camping?

All I know is he should have been taking me with him. The lady hooman says something about "No way I'm going camping. Sleeping outside is too cold." I agree with her, sounds like sleeping in the kennel. Who the heck would want to do that?

Maybe he wasn't a good boy and the lady hooman made him

sleep outside? Ooo you're in trouble now hooman! Is that why you made that shed thing? I know I'll go check, maybe he is in there! (Checks), nope he's not there.

I guess I'll have to settle for the girl hooman and the lady hooman...I miss my hooman...please come back to me hooman. You don't have to sleep outside!

GUNNER'S PERSON HERE

A lot of this had to be relayed by my wife and my daughter. My son and I have been involved with Scouts for years and have gone camping once a month or nearly so year after year. What Gunner was going through is from what I understand, a fairly common occurrence once we leave the house.

Often times he gets really antsy on Thursday night as he has learned that once we start bringing up our gear and leaving it the back living room, soon it will be time for me to go. One Friday morning I found him sprawled across my sleeping bag and gear. Either he was telling me not to go or scent marking my gear to let other dogs know I belong to him. Who really knows what goes through a dog's mind though. Suffice to say he wasn't happy when we left.

One also has to wonder what they think when we don't come back home when we normally would do so? It's a guess they tell time through smell. That is to say they can gauge time based on the decreasing intensity of scents. And when they know the scent of their favorite person is at a certain point it means they should be home. And when that doesn't happen? Likely it's panic time in the doggy mind or quite possible frantic time!

In some ways, I actually do feel really bad. Gunner is not a young dog and one weekend a month I'm away from him for a good chunk of the weekend, at least from Friday night to late

Sunday morning. In one respect it makes it better when I get to see him. There he is eagerly awaiting our return and relieved that we are back. For the next few hours or even a day or so, I've noticed he is more attached to me than normal; worried I'm going to be gone again. Not going to lie, it is heartwarming he misses me so much.

PANDEMIC, WHAT THE HECK IS THAT?

3-10-20

GUNNER THE BEAGLE HERE!

The hoomans look very concerned, they keeping saying the word "pandemic." I have no idea what the heck that is. I do know there has been a change. Normally during the day I have to go inside my crate. It's still nice in there and lots of soft blankets, although the lady hooman washes them from time to time saying it "smells like dog" well duh, of course, I'm a dog! Anyways, the smaller hoomans seem to be home all the time now, sometimes my hooman too. That means I don't have to go in my crate during the day?

He keeps saying "Gunner wanna go to work?" He looks at me and we head downstairs to the man cave like we do most nights. But then we have dinner and go back down there again! It's like double the time with my hooman!

I'm getting so comfortable in my bed down there I woke up drooling. My hooman was laughing. I didn't find it funny!

GUNNER'S PERSON HERE

Like most everyone we have no idea what this pandemic will bring. Kids are home with remote learning and I'm working from home a lot as well. Gunner, like I suspect a lot of pets, is happy we are home a lot more and he doesn't have to go into the crate during the day.

Timber, as always, is unimpressed as she hasn't had to be crated during the day in years.

In any event, after breakfast I tell him it is indeed time for work and we head downstairs. He's my coworker now in addition to my dog. He loves the routine and serves as a reminder to get up and move from time to time when he has to go outside. And the drooling part? I happened to look over and he was sound asleep on his back with all paws in the air like usual and sure enough, drooling. It was rather funny actually.

As it's still on the cool side being late winter here. I have the space heater set up for him near his bed. He is really happy about this, and every once in a while gets up, circles and places his other side near the heat.

During the day he serves as my clock. It's not that I can't use my watch or phone for time, but I get used to his need to go outside to mark the hours. He also seems to know when it's lunch time. One has to wonder if dogs smell the changes in us during the day and know what time it is roughly.

RUNNING AROUND THE YARD
4-11-20

GUNNER THE BEAGLE HERE!

It's been a very fun day! The white stuff is gone and it's squishy outside and it's really a mess in the yard my hooman says. But I don't care! The boy hooman is running around the yard and I'm chasing him! Just like I used to chase Bandit. Oh, I hope Bandit is good! Oh, I get this. The boy hooman is a rabbit. I'm a beagle. I'm supposed to chase those down being a beagle and all. (Huff, huff) The back yard is really big!

The small hooman keeps saying "treat" and of course I have to chase after him! I wonder why Timber isn't chasing after him? Maybe she knows something I don't? Doesn't matter, remember he's the rabbit!

I have to take a break and rest, I'm not young anymore. My hoomans say I just turned twelve? I have no idea what twelve is. I do know that I get tired more quickly now. I still like running around the yard though.

Anyways back at it, get back here small hooman before I get tired again!

GUNNER'S PERSON HERE

It was a fun day for the boy and Gunner. Gunner is too old for zoomies around the yard, but he does like to run on occasion.

My son likes to give him treats and how does he get Gunner to run? He runs around with them and Gunner chases after him and my son slows down enough for Gunner to "catch" him. So in a way it really is like Gunner is chasing down those rabbits that he sees in the yard from time to time (the back fence borders some high brush).

He has just turned twelve and is still fairly spry for his age. He does get tired easily and I tell my son to take it easy on Gunner and not tire him out too much. At his age, one of my concerns is a major leg injury. We take him for walks sure, but running around the yard is something else entirely.

I like to believe that part of his running around is the feeling of freedom. As Gunner is a smaller dog, from his perspective the back yard is really big, lots of places for him to roam and run. While not completely free, he likely has more freedom now then he has ever had in the past. It all goes back to we can't know for sure all the details of his previous living conditions, but the pieces we know? We'll leave it at that. Then again, maybe I'm completely off on all of this and he roamed around wherever he wanted in his previous life, at least I hope he did.

Regardless of the past, my son and Gunner had a great, albeit muddy, day. I'm sure as the weather improves there will be more of these days ahead. That thought brings a smile to our faces because we know that something so simple is the whole world to Gunner.

WALKS ARE MY FAVORITE!

5-12-20

GUNNER THE BEAGLE HERE!

The hoomans all seem to be outside these days and walking around. My hoomans have been taking me for a lot more of them as well. The weather is warm, I like that. Timber can't figure it out either. Something about "the pandemic still going on?" Still have no clue what that is. But Timber and I don't care, we are out on a walk!

We see lots of other hoomans with their dogs too. Sometimes we go up and say hi to the other dogs while the hoomans talk to each other, from a distance. The other dogs are all saying the same thing: How great this pandemic thing is and how their hoomans are home a lot more too! Everyone is happy, except for those dogs that also have cats at home. The other dogs say that the cats are all grumpy because people are home. Cats are weird. We don't have any cats at home.

Either way, it's getting even warmer and my hoomans are with me! I really like it when we walk when there is no white stuff, better to wee-wee on stuff! Timber is looking all goofy. She's happy to be out walking too.

Our hoomans put these things called "bandannas" on Timber and I. All the other hoomans think we look cute, well duh hoomans, of course we are! Silly hoomans.

GUNNER'S PERSON HERE

Like a lot of people, the world is still unsettled and no one knows what to make of the contagion going on. Everything is shut down or being canceled.

As a result Gunner and Timber are getting a lot more walks. Timber is not shaggy and sporting a nice new bandanna, so we got one for Gunner too.

Walking Gunner at first presented a lot of unknowns. Had he ever even gone on a walk prior was our biggest question. He quickly got the hang of it and surprised us by being able to pad right along Timber without slowing down unless to stop and sniff. He has come a long way since when we first got him and he would tug at the leash and lean into it. Now, a few years later he is an old pro at it.

He gets excited and begins to get fidgety when the word "walk" is spoken and sees the leash. Of course, this isn't anything out of the ordinary and all dogs likely go through the same excitement. I think the part that brought it home for me was walking both dogs, my wife and I realized how much better it was than just one. It took no time at all and Timber seemed to like having someone else to walk with as much as we do.

In all though, a dog walk is a simple pleasure and one that is in a lot of ways relaxing, at least for the most part. Dogs want very little from us and the highlight of their day? To simply walk around and smell stuff with their humans in tow. Life for humans would likely be a whole lot better if we understood such simple things and take them for what they are. Dogs get this.

CRUNCHY GREEN STICKS?

6-13-20

GUNNER THE BEAGLE HERE!

My hoomans think they can fool me. They left out some food where I could get it. I waited till they weren't looking and I swiped it! I made off with my prize (Timber was sleeping). I had it all to myself and sniffed, hmm orange crunchy sticks? I like these things, I'll snack on those!

(Sniffs again) hey what are these green sticks? They don't really smell like anything? Alright I'll try one. Yuck! These things taste awful. They taste worse anything! I think they taste worse than socks after Timber is done sucking on them! Ugh those are the worse. Doggy toothpaste for you Timber!

Oh no, what am I going to do with these green sticks? Maybe if I just leave it here in the corner no one will notice I ate their "vegetable tray" or whatever they called it. Wait a minute, they might notice that some of the orange sticks are gone, maybe I can blame that one on Timber!

Oh no better get out of here. I hear the hoomans coming back inside from the garage thing...

GUNNER'S PERSON HERE

The pandemic continues to ratchet up the lock downs and we figured what the heck, we'll get some vegetables while we sit outside and soak up the sun with drinks and the dogs lounging around. We were outside looking at something and both dogs were inside. Little did we know that our beagle buddy was helping himself to snacks. We have given both dogs carrots as a snack to vary it up from the other treats. Both like them, I suspect the crunch of them has something to do with it.

That may have been why he thought it was fine to help himself to more.

But imagine Gunner's surprise when he got to, you guessed it, celery. He was not impressed at all and while he did grab a few, he spit them out soon after trying as near as we can tell. Timber far wiser had rejected them a long time ago. I can only imagine the dog conversations the two had. I imagine her laughing as he tried them, knowing what they taste like.

Chopped up in a salad? Then celery is fine. But just sticks of them? Not even with dip makes them all that appealing. Seriously, does anyone actively seek out celery on a party tray as the first thing to eat? And for dogs, it has to really be a let down. They are omnivores meaning they will eat almost anything. But when a dog passes on celery? Sorry celery, it's not your fault that Gunner was not a fan, and well almost anyone really.

EVERYTHING BEAGLE

7-23-20

GUNNER THE BEAGLE HERE!

My hooman is at it again, instead of big ears or antlers, he bought me a shirt? A shirt? What the heck? I can't eat a shirt! Or maybe I can, never tried that. Anyways, I hope you don't think I'm actually going to wear that? I have fur, remember silly hooman? On top of this, you usually do these on those things you call "holidays." This isn't a holiday is it?

MOMENTS IN TIME

THE RIDE HOME 12-12-18

This is the day we brought him home. Gunner is smiling a big grin here as is plain to see. From living outside in a kennel, then to the shelter, then to his forever home. Perhaps he knew even then that he was our dog.

HOME AT LAST
12-12-18

This is in the evening of his first day home. He's already settled in and already looking for food in the kitchen.

MY HELPER 8-29-19

Here is my "helper" during the construction of the shed. He and I had a bond from the beginning, but it was on this day we became inseparable; wherever I went he had to go too. It was around this time we started calling him my barnacle.

WHO ME? 3-28-20

This is the photo that adorned my lock screen on my phone for years. I got this shot on the third take. First two? Not so good, but on the third one, he looked right at me as if to say "take the photo already!"

CONTENT 5-9-20

As he did on many a night, this is typical of my buddy. Being older, Gunner was simply content to be near me in whatever I might happen to be doing. Here he is in the man cave snoozing away.

TREATS 12-22-20

Timber and Gunner in the kitchen sitting nicely for treats. Timber was seven when Gunner came to us and Gunner was almost 11. The two of them got along well and never fought. In fact, he often bossed her around and she would just go with it.

("Oof"), my hooman is having a hard time putting this thing on me. The lady hooman is laughing, saying something about "it must have shrunk." Then my hooman says something about I'm still carrying a little "holiday extra weight." They are laughing again. Hey, I don't make fun of your "holiday weight" hooman, whatever that is.

He's still struggling to put it on me. I'm not laughing, but they are snickering.

Now they have those phone things out and are taking pictures of me. I hope they don't let anyone else see these photo things.

Usually with these things I get treats for this. How about steak!

GUNNER'S PERSON HERE

It is out of character for me to do something like this, usually the ears or antlers is for holidays, it makes sense and he is fine with it. Buying a dog shirt is a bit out there.

FOR HIM THERE IS ONLY NOW. AND FOR HIM, HIS NOW IS PERFECT.

While I was at the pet shop, I found a dog shirt that says "I'm your everything bagel" with the picture of an everything bagel on it. Of course having a beagle, it meant something different to us. He's our "Everything Beagle." Imagine my surprise when I actually bought it. Still surprising to me that I did it.

And Gunner is correct: it is a bit...ahem..."snug" on certain portions for him...In the years since he left the shelter, his weight has come down a bit. Not that he was massively overweight, but with beagles they can be overweight, especially as they age, so we make sure to monitor him.

He allowed me to put it on him without any real issues and while it probably wasn't his favorite thing, (he squirmed a bit) he tolerated it. As we snapped photos, I thought about how perfect dogs are, particularly Gunner. Gunner had every reason to be closed off and withdrawn. He had every right to not be friendly, but he is. And here he is putting a doggy t-shirt on him with no protest.

All he ever wanted was to be with people and to be loved. When I look at him, I see so much that we could have done for him had we had him from the beginning and it makes me sad. At the same time, he doesn't think about it, for him there is only now. And for him, his now is perfect.

It's an amazing lesson that I've learned from my furry friend who I didn't even know existed a few years before. Live for now because tomorrow is not assured.

SNACKING IN THE GARDEN
8-20-20

GUNNER THE BEAGLE HERE!

It's been really hot here and even too much for me if I'm not in the shade. I sometimes sit outside with the other hooman in the sun. She reads something called a book and I hide out under her chair or the table.

My hooman isn't here today and all this stuff has grown from the ground. There are those crunchy orange sticks and other stuff. They keep calling it a garden. Looks like a lot of weeds to me. I should go wee-wee on them!

I wander through the garden and my hooman tries to shoo me away. Does he know just who I am? No way hooman, I'm going in here to see if there are snacks!

Hmm what are these small yellow things? They smell okay, chomp!

GUNNER'S PERSON HERE

As the pandemic rolls on, the garden continues to grow and is producing vegetables. Gunner, our food overdrive beagle, is of course, looking for food. Keeping a close eye on him as he has to go explore. And no matter what, he disappears into the thicker bushes and finds the ripe, yellow pear tomatoes.

Now I know what you might be thinking: no unripened tomatoes for dogs. Unfortunately before we can get him out he snacks on a bunch of them. It is rather amusing as he exits the garden with yellow stains on his nearly white face.

I'm struck with two thoughts, the first is the lengths he will go to for food. There are even more extreme measures he does, tomatoes are mild in comparison. I'm at a loss at the moment that after two years with us he is still worried about his next meal.

The second part I dwell on is just how white he has gotten. His face is really white now, his ears and coat on his back have lot of white streaked throughout. His socks on his paws have disappeared and now he has four all white limbs. Time has passed quickly, too quickly. In December, it will be two years since we brought him home and in some ways it seems like a blink of an eye.

Over the next few days, he makes more forays into the garden despite our best efforts to keep him out. We eventually resort to a lead so he can't get all the way back there. Of course, the kids aren't as careful as we are, and invariably we find him at the door with a yellow stained face. We keep an eye on him and no symptoms. I have seen him eat far worse than tomatoes. Echos from his time before us maybe, and ones I don't want to dwell on.

He is a typical beagle through and through all this. And for those that don't know, what sound does a beagle make when they are getting into trouble? The answer: none at all.

WARMING IN THE SUN

9-5-20

GUNNER THE BEAGLE HERE!

A long while ago my person built a shed, I remember I remember! I helped! He says it is used to "store stuff." At least it's not a dog house. I still say it looks like one.

The ramp is my favorite part. The ramp gets warm in the mornings. I've been laying on it in the mornings to get warm, just like I used to try and get warm with Bandit. I miss him. I hope he is alright. It's just the right size for me to flop down on and stretch out.

My hooman is looking at me funny from inside, smiling about something. I hope it doesn't mean he is going to try and give me a bath...or antlers or that shirt again???

Maybe I should scamper off, nah, I'll just keep an eye on him and stay here…ZZZ...

GUNNER'S PERSON HERE

It's an early Saturday morning and my wife is at work. The kids are sleeping, as is Timber. Gunner and I are the only ones up. The weather hasn't quite yet started to turn cold here, but it is getting damp at night, even in early September. Today is warm though, one of those late summer/early fall days that is perfect.

He goes outside after eating and does his business. From there he pads right over to the shed and stretches out and positions himself looking at me by the sliding glass doors. He has his head on his paws and he just keeps looking. He's content and I simply let him stay there for about an hour checking on him periodically.

As I look at him I wonder at his past life. Is he missing Bandit? Does he sense and feel the changes in the weather, knowing that the cold rainy autumn is on its way, followed by the sometimes downright frigid winters? Is he trying to warm himself as much as he can before the weather turns? Does he know that warming up heralds something more?

Or maybe I'm simply projecting, that he's not thinking these things and it's as simple as he's outside and he is warm. As I gaze at him through the window, I don't feel I need to go to him, nor does he seem to feel the need to get up and come inside. It's strange, but for a bit, we just look at each other, each content and happy. I'm happy that he is safe and right there. I do have to wonder though, is he happy if for no other reason then I am?

It doesn't matter if any of that is the case between Gunner and I. On this day, I know we are both happy just to be with each other.

DREAMING AGAIN

10-5-20

GUNNER THE BEAGLE HERE!

ZZZ…I'm running fast, just like I used to do when I was young, or at least when I was allowed to! ZZZ…

Where did that rabbit go? There he is! I must go faster to catch him! How come I can't catch him? My legs are going really, really fast, but he keeps getting away! Am I even moving at all?

What's going on now? It's suddenly swirly and cloudy and now there is a blue sky and I see all my paws in the air? I must be on my back. Suddenly chicken and steaks are floating in the air, they are waiting for me to snatch them and make off with them! I want them, give them to me! ZZZ...

Got them, my belly is full and I'm sleeping warm and cozy! Now I just need some doggy ice cream...

ZZZ........

GUNNER'S PERSON HERE

Even more so then a few months back, Gunner is in the throws of a doggy dream. He dreams nearly all the time and as he has gotten older, they seem to get more intense. Also as dogs age the mechanism that prevents them from acting out their dreams wanes and they are more reflexive. Certainly for us, he is the most vivid dreamer of any dog we have ever had.

From the look of it he is having an intense dream, perhaps the most intense one I have seen. He is twitching and whimpering more than we have ever seen him do. Yet no growls or anything untold. His legs are all twitching wildly and it looks as if he is trying to run (and chase) after something.

And that is all part of doggy dreams. Some nights it's one of the best things ever to just watch Gunner as he sleeps very deeply. Other nights it's nothing at all but that is the exception rather than the rule. I find myself wondering: dreams about what though? Who knows what dogs truly dream about, although it's been said that it's things they enjoy while awake: playing catch, chasing squirrels and rabbits, or just being with their favorite people.

We're lucky he doesn't have nightmares and at least from the outside looking in, he's happy. In this he's a beagle through and through. Once he has really settled in, he will usually sleep on his back with all four paws in the air and a happy, almost grin on his face. Of course the legs start twitching and he starts making noises. I've recorded him plenty of times when he's dreaming as I do so again tonight. It never gets old.

Eventually he settles into a deep sleep. I hope his dreams are great and he is having the time of his life. From the look of it, he's completely content. His grin couldn't be any wider and neither could mine. We get to see him sleep all the time and never think anything about it. But this time really caught my attention and makes my whole week.

TURKEY DAY?

11-25-20

GUNNER THE BEAGLE HERE!

The lady hooman got up really early and started cooking. The smells were great all morning! Timber says today is one of the best days, because we get extra fud! Something called Thanksgiving or "Turkey Day?" Oh yeah, I remember this! Wait… it's one of them holiday things. You guys better not have some ear things for me to wear!

My person left as he said something to the lady hooman of "I can't, I've got to go to work." That's okay hooman, Timber and I will keep her company while she is cooking! It also means he's not putting something on me! Maybe she'll drop something and I can pounce on it before Timber…

In what seems like forever, my hooman finally comes home from that work thing. I go to the door and greet him, mainly so we can eat! Hurry up hooman! The lady hooman says "everything is ready and it's time to eat." The best part? We get some of the turkey too!

Later when they are eating something called "dessert" we get bones and some pumpkin instead. I'm not sure why we can't have what they are having, but Timber and I take our big bones and head off. The pumpkin stuff was good too.

GUNNER'S PERSON HERE

As my wife usually works on Thanksgiving, we celebrate it on Wednesday. This works out great because on the actual day when she gets home, we have leftovers and watch football. We started this tradition last year and so it is again.

While we're all settled and everyone is content. I take a moment to observe the dogs. Timber in her bed and Gunner in his "nest" as we call it. Usually, I take stock at Christmas, but it strikes me about the idea of Thanksgiving and being thankful, for which I am. I have the best beagle anyone could ask for, our golden girl Timber, and we're all safe and healthy. The dogs have worked over their marrow bones for a while and are now snoozing.

I get up during a break in the game and glance outside. It's so dark now and a bit of wisps of snow; nothing major and nothing staying on the ground. I glance to Gunner in his nest: he's curled up and sleeping soundly. It's a great ending to the day.

Turns out I have another surprise for him: I don't have to work on Friday. So, my son and I will be watching college football and pro games throughout this weekend, and Gunner won't have to be pining for me at the door.

-2021-
MY EYE IS ITCHY
1-3-21

GUNNER THE BEAGLE HERE!

My person better get with it. My eye is all itchy and my hooman is looking at it concerned. You're the smart hooman, fix it you dummy! What, you can't FIX IT RIGHT NOW?

I'm pawing at it and everything. He doesn't get it. Maybe if I give him the "head tilt" that will do it.

Still nothing.

Hey… wait. He's got something in his hands and he's saying "it's for your own good." Now he's saying to the lady hooman something called "eye drops?"

LET ME OUT OF HERE! YOU'RE NOT DOING ANYTHING WITH THAT!

"Oof," he got me. I'm not making this easy!

GUNNER'S PERSON HERE

In December we noticed another skin bump on his left eyelid. Having gone through the scare a few years back with his eye, we got him checked out at the Vet. Fortunately, she says it's most likely non-cancerous, but we need an eye specialist to do the surgery. The procedure is fairly simple: the surgeon will basically freeze it off.

The problem? The Pandemic has backed up surgeries for dogs just like for humans. I make an appointment, but I can't get him in till the end of March. In the meantime, I have to try a variety of different treatments to get him there: ointment and drops.

The other problem? Unlike last time, it's a bit on the outside and inside of his left eyelid. I can't imagine it's all that comfortable for him so I have to try and treat it the best I can.

As anyone can imagine the challenge of trying to administer medication to a squirmy beagle who has no inclination to help is difficult in the best of times. Rather than try to force it when he knows it's coming, I have to get sneaky: a senior dog sleeps a lot. Hence, I can "ambush" him when he least expects it. I have to be wary as he is fairly smart and I don't want him to associate it with anything bad so I try to administer the drops when he is deep in sleep and try to avoid his safe places like the man cave or his crate.

I wish I could do more, but I can't make time go any faster. All I can do is keep a watch on his eye and hope it's not bothering him too much.

MY EYE IS FIXED!

3-30-21

GUNNER THE BEAGLE HERE!

We went for a really long ride this time and it looks like we're at another shelter? What gives hooman, I live with you, don't forget that? He says it's some sort of clinic and we are "early." That's fine get me out of the truck and I can go wee-wee on stuff and sniff around here!

It's now time and a nice lady comes to the door! Let me in! Maybe the nice shelter ladies are in there and I can say hi!

Except it's not and my hooman has to wait outside, wait...I'm scared without my hooman here. But the other hoomans here are really nice, they keep looking at my eye. Oh yeah, before we set out today my hooman said they were going to fix it, he must mean this place. It's really scratchy and itchy, maybe they really can do something to fix it? I trust my hooman though, he always knows! Good hooman!

ZZZ...

I went to sleep and I woke up with this really big cone on me and I don't know why. I feel really loopy too. But my eye feels a lot better. Hey, what the heck is this cone thing around my neck! I don't like this thing, take it off hooman!

It's now time for the truck ride home? My hooman picks me up ("oof") and I still don't feel so good. I usually like the rides when he picks me up but this is different. My breathing is really, really crazy! Maybe I can sleep some more and it will all feel better.

GUNNER'S PERSON HERE

Today Gunner had eye surgery for a lump on his left eyelid. We have had it scheduled for months, but were finally able to get in due the backlog of surgeries due to the Pandemic. Turns out it was non-cancerous and it was really annoying for him. He would paw at it and rub his face on the ground. I'm sure it didn't feel good.

The Veterinary surgeon said she got all of the growth out and it should not return.

The biggest concern was him coming out of surgery at 13 years old. He was very disoriented and breathing heavily from the experience. I was concerned that he might not make it, but thankfully he did. There is always a risk with any dog in surgery and more so given his age. Either way it's not something I want

Gunner to go through again, for his sake obviously and somewhat mine as well.

He is not a fan of the cone to keep him from getting at his eye. He doesn't try to take it off so maybe he is just putting up with it.

Through it all though I got one very special gift. We had to get there early and the clinic is one and half hours from our house. As always I scooped him up and off we went. The best part though? About thirty minutes into the ride as we got on the Interstate he shifted around in the passenger seat, and lay largely across the console so he could be in touch with me as we drove. I looked at him, eyes closed and so serene knowing that all he wanted was to be near me. That's the power of dogs: they really don't want much and what they give is far more.

And on this day he gave me everything I ever needed. My heart is full.

BATH TIME AGAIN?

6-22-21

GUNNER THE BEAGLE HERE!

I AM NOT HAPPY WITH MY HOOMAN!

We went for a truck ride and I love those! But my hooman tricked me, he brought me to a pet store. Not sure what those are as I'm a dog. I thought I hit the jackpot as he was giving me lots of treats, there were lots of those around...but he wouldn't let me get into the big bins! What gives hooman!

But what does he do instead? He scoops me up ("oof") and puts me in a tub with water? I don't swim. I only doggy paddle!

What's this? BATH TIME, NO WAY! I just had one, well I did have one…I just don't remember when though…Anyways I wanted out and he wouldn't let me so I used my latent super power, my beagle howl, that will show him! Aryooo!

This time my hooman, does not know! Bad hooman! (Don't tell him I'm really not that mad at him, I can never be mad at my hooman!)

Good he got me out and now it's time for my revenge! Time to shake all the water off on him! There that did it! He's got a strange look on his face, better do it again!

THAT WILL SHOW YOU HOOMAN! Now, where are the treats?

GUNNER'S PERSON HERE

You would have thought they were handing out awards for best acting. Someone decided that this was the place to discover his acting talents: the dog wash stations at the pet store. You also would have also thought there was complete pandemonium going on in there from the racket. And you'd be right. The store and its patrons were treated to a masterclass piece of theater as he barked, howled, squirmed, tugged, whined, and cried.

Baths have always been a challenge with him. Interestingly enough, he doesn't have that much of a dog smell. My wife disagrees and says he does get that dog funk. Maybe my sense of smell isn't as good or because I'm so close to him all the time that I just don't notice it.

I figured this time it might just be easier to bathe him at the store than the mess that usually results from when we try to do it at home.

I figured wrong.

WANDERING AWAY FROM HOME!

8-1-21

GUNNER THE BEAGLE HERE!

My hooman wasn't watching so I was able to make an escape for it! I slipped through the gate when they weren't looking and went exploring for food. I made it quite a way from my hoomans, some nice, other hoomans said "look how cute he is!" They were so nice, they pet me and were making a big fuss over me! I like this! I gave them the side head tilt, that usually does it and maybe I'll get treats!

Looks like this wandering thing is worth it. One of the new hoomans is going into one of those garage things to get the goods! The nice hooman keeps petting me!

They were getting ready to keep me and then my hooman showed up. He looked very happy to see me, I think I'll stay with my hooman, at least for now. Although these other hoomans did say something about treats, but it doesn't look like he has any with him? What gives hooman?

Okay fine, we'll go home and I leave these nice hoomans... for now.

GUNNER'S PERSON HERE

Not a good feeling. One of the issues with Gunner is he is so food driven and he doesn't make a lot of noise when he is out looking for food. He's stealthy like that, plus a low profile. When the fence first went up, he made it out by slipping under a low spot which I didn't think he could get through. Fixed that and he found one more, fixed that too.

When Timber has gotten out, she doesn't usually go too far and only my daughter can get her to come back. For the rest of us, it's a lost cause as she just runs away like it's a game.

Our sneaky little guy, on the other hand, made it halfway down the street, a good way from our house. The problem? His name tag and phone number had fallen off and we hadn't noticed. There was that pit in the stomach feeling of just where is he? He's older and could have gotten anywhere. What if he went to the back fields? Despite the fence I know there are coyotes not too far away and he's a senior dog and not too fast...

We fanned out and started looking for him. I put myself in his mindset and figured which way he would most likely go. Sure enough he was the direction I thought he would go and was visiting with some neighbors quite a ways from our house. I talked to them and they laughed. They said, and I quote, "We were ready to keep him, he's so cute!" No way guys, he's mine!

I herded him back to our house and he didn't even think twice about wandering. That sneaky guy got out and didn't even give a second glance backwards! What does he do? Goes inside and flops in his bed and sleeps...apparently that was enough exploring for one day.

TRUCK RIDE, MY FAVORITE!

9-4-21

GUNNER THE BEAGLE HERE!

Today was the best! My hooman brought me out the front of the house and I thought we were going for a walk! Nope, turns out it was a truck ride! Are we going to a shelter again? Or are we going somewhere else?

My hooman picks me up to get in the truck ("oof"). I like it when he picks me up, he does my bidding! Plus I get to smell him, I like his smell. Even better, I get to tell other dogs he's mine!

Some dogs like to stick their heads out the window when the hoomans drive them around. Not me, I like to curl up in ball and sleep. My hooman is nearby and we are in his truck, this is the best. Some times he makes the seats warm too! Smart hooman! Other times he pets me. I like that too!

The best part of the truck rides is I get to spend time with just my hooman. I like the other hoomans in the pack, but I like him the best! Plus we stop places and he lets me out to go wee-wee on stuff!

(Sniff, sniff) smells good around here but the trees are starting to smell different. I think they know the white stuff will be falling soon.

GUNNER'S PERSON HERE

Gunner lives for his truck rides here and there. Aside from food, it's one of his favorite things. Ever since we got him a few years back, he and I would just go for random rides in the truck, just Gunner and I. And even now, it's something that he eagerly looks forward to and something that he and I are the only ones to share.

Sometimes I talk to him and other times we just drive in silence with just the sound of the wind through the windows. Every once in a while he opens an eye to make sure I'm still there. Don't worry buddy, I always will be, now and forever.

The weather is starting to get a bit cooler at night already and the air crisper. That means football is around the corner where he will nestle into his bed on Sundays and more truck rides as I love the fall. Driving around with him in my favorite season is one of the simple things in life that I wouldn't trade for the world. Sometimes we get out when he has to go to the bathroom and I lead him off and let him go sniff after he is done. He seems to very much understand the change of the seasons owing to his past life. The leaves here won't change color for a bit but some of the early ones are starting to fall.

We get back in and I sing songs to him very softly and he doesn't to mind my bad singing voice. We continue on for about another hour and then turn for home. I tell him "we're home" and he opens an eye and looks at me as if to say, "Well, sure you dummy we're home, but home for me is when we are together." Okay maybe I just thought that's what it meant but thinking upon it, there isn't anything I wouldn't do to keep him with me and well...home.

SLEEPING NEXT TO MY PERSON!

10-9-21

GUNNER THE BEAGLE HERE!

I've moved from my regular bed to sleeping next to my hooman! Oh boy, he's warm and I like to lay next to him, just like I did with Bandit, but better. My hooman is very warm! Sometimes I flop down next to Timber, but she can get grumpy when I take over her bed. What gives, it's not your bed, it's mine! You just sleep here when I let you!

The lady hooman didn't like it when I lay across her legs and would squirm. I was really trying to get my hooman all to myself! Shhh don't tell her. Maybe if I try and nudge her she'll fall out of the bed! Better do it stealthy!

The lady hooman says this isn't working and my hooman picks me up ("oof") and carries me downstairs and sets up something called a "fold out bed?" There are a lot of blankets and stuff and I get to curl up next to my hooman! This is what I wanted all along! They never suspected I could be so sneaky and I got away with it!

Timber is looking at us strangely! No way Timber I'm not sharing him with you!

Wait, what was I saying...ZZZ...

GUNNER'S PERSON HERE

I'm hoping this is temporary. Lately he cannot settle down at night and him sleeping in our bed didn't work. He actually tried (or so it seems) to muscle my wife off the bed and it isn't working. At first, he starts out by laying largely next to me, then eventually ends up on her. Taking one for the team, I bring him downstairs.

The old boy and I are down to the fold out bed. For the two of us, it's old comforters and some sleeping bags and blankets. I get settled in and at first he is curled up in a ball nearby on the bed keeping an eye on me. But eventually he moves over and lays lengthwise on my left side. Almost as if he wanted this all along: sleeping next to me and no one else. I'm fairly certain this was his plan.

Timber is good about it as she has always slept nearby, but never right with us. In fact, she has always slept downstairs at the foot of the stairs usually. She opens an eye when we come downstairs, lifts her head briefly and goes back to sleep as if to say "this is all you two."

My hope for one night seems to be a pipe dream, over the next few nights he gets used to this. Just what have I gotten myself into? But if I'm honest I have the best beagle in the world who wants nothing more than to be by my side always. Certainly, that is not a bad thing. Not a bad thing at all.

A BIG PILE OF SMELL

11-14-21

GUNNER THE BEAGLE HERE!

The lady hooman thwarted my plans! Don't ask me what that means as I'm a dog, we just do, no planning! Anyways my hooman and the boy hooman went camping again. I really don't like it when they leave, my hooman goes away from me! At least he could bring me too? I heard they sleep outside on the ground so maybe not, I had enough of that! Anyways they just got back.

There was a big pile of those clothes things they wear, from both of them! I really, really liked it; it smelled smoky and sweaty! Then the lady hooman found more in something called a "gym bag" and was complaining to my hooman. Hey lady, he's mine, you don't get to do that! Anyways, she said something about all these things stink! What? No way lady, these things smell great!

Now it's time to wiggle around on the top of the pile.

Ugh, now she is putting them in something called a washing machine? Hey that's like when I get a bath! I hate those, then another weird thing called a dryer? At least they are warm when she takes them out...

Hey, these smell weird now, what gives!

GUNNER'S PERSON HERE

Dogs are such amazing, and at the same time, wonderfully weird creatures to us humans. Imagine my surprise when my wife called me to the laundry room and there was Gunner on a pile of mine and my son's clothing from our last campout. Several days of camp clothes coupled with some gym clothing that I "forgot" to remove from my bag? So what does Gunner do? He decides that the pile is the perfect place to "beach" himself. There he is all spread out rolling around in them much like when a dog finds a dead fish on the beach.

When my wife found him on the pile, he had a look of "Yeah? So what?" Personally, I wonder if he was searching for (likely) food my son left in a pocket by "accident."

Now the clothing wasn't as bad as my wife says it was...but it's still somewhat amazing that after just a shade under three years with us, he can't seem to get enough of smelly stuff and more importantly my scent on said clothing. We've found him before laying on stuff of mine, but he seemed especially pleased with himself today. Timber doesn't do this. She used to mouth dirty socks, but not nest in dirty clothes.

I put myself in his mindset and imagined just how reassuring this is to him. Reassuring, but likely it's also an experience that humans with our lesser senses of smell can't understand in the way dogs do. Smell is their "language" in the same way sight is for us. He knows my son and I were gone for several days, but in a way, he could tell a lot about what we had been doing...the smell of the smoke from the campfire, who was with us, and what we had been cooking. I don't think I'm too far off. Some of the best tracking hounds, of which beagles are can detect smells over hours and days. So for him to figure it out after being away for just two days?

Of course, I could be way off on this, but from the look of him on top of the pile of clothes? He seems to be quite happy with it.

CHRISTMAS 2021

12-12-21

GUNNER THE BEAGLE HERE!

What the heck is this? Why am I the one who always gets dressed up? How about Timber for a change? Reindeer antlers? I have to wear them? Well, okay but only if I get treats for this! Huh, you put them on already? I can't really feel them. Still doesn't matter, I'm doing this under protest!

Great, now I have to sit still while they take photos with those phone things? Fine. I'll do it, but better make it quick! Ugh, now some photos on the staircase? In the kitchen too. C'mon hurry up already!

There I wore them! Now hand over the snacks! Wait...I only get the crunchy orange sticks for this? You can do better than that hoomans. You also keep saying it's been three years since I "came home" like a celebration? You better be making me some steak!

GUNNER'S PERSON HERE

Another anniversary of Gunner being brought home has arrived and we are blessed to have him in our lives. Another year of a great Christmas gift and one to be thankful for. Unfortunately for him, it also means antlers for photos which he tolerates as he always does as I take photos of him.

It's been three years since we brought Gunner home, to his true home, being the greatest thing we have ever done. In some ways it seems like a blink of an eye, in others it seems like he has always been here. Sure it feels good for us, but for him? It changed his life and his golden years are filled with people around him, food, warmth, and love. We truly can't imagine life without him.

When one is younger, Christmas is about what you get. One could look at him the same way I suppose. We "got" him right before Christmas 2018. But being a dog, Gunner has given far more than we could ever give him.

My hope for this Christmas is many more with a truly ancient beagle in the years to come, curled up by the heat, and one I have to gently awaken to carry outside and to bed. It's the simple things like this I hope for at the holidays for him and I. That he can grow ever older, sleeping more and content to be with us.

I never had a chance to do that with any of my other dogs due to the circumstances of their passing. I hope that for Gunner it's a final gift I'll be able to give him when the time comes after always being there for us.

LIFE CHANGES IN AN INSTANT

1-27-22

GUNNER THE BEAGLE HERE!

My hooman is acting weird, something about my sniffer feels not quite right. My hooman looks very worried. What the heck is with that? He talks to the hooman lady and she seems concerned too.

We go outside, Oh boy a truck ride, he picks me up ("oof") and we go for a short ride. Looks like the shelter! Let me inside to see the nice shelter ladies! I try to get in back but they smell different. Nope it's not the shelter.

The dog doctor is a nice lady and she looks at my sniffer and my hooman is really concerned and upset again? I hope he's not upset with me? He's petting me softly and talking to the dog doctor.

DON'T WORRY HOOMAN, IT'S PROBABLY NOTHING. IT DOES FEEL A BIT DIFFERENT, BUT MY SNIFFER WORKS!

As we leave he begins to talk to me and cry. He says something about that small bump on my snout? Don't worry hooman, it's probably nothing. It does feel a bit different, but my sniffer works!

GUNNER'S PERSON HERE

Some moments in life will always stand out as to the when and where, of how you'll never forget that type of life changing news. Today was that day. Today I learned that my buddy, my heart and soul, has maybe three to maybe five months left to live.

It started in late December 2021. We noticed a small lump growing on the right side of his snout somewhat close to but not on his eye. Scheduling and perhaps some dread meant I couldn't get him there immediately. The Vet told us: he has a small cancerous bump on the right side of his snout. There is no curing this, you can only delay it and that is really only with younger dogs. Gunner will be fourteen in March.

Add to this his reaction to the surgery from March of 2021 and nearly a year older? It's not good no matter how one looks at it. Even if we opt for surgery, will he come out of it? Add to this younger dogs have a greater chance of doing well. He's not young anymore, and even then, it only delays it. With dogs, nasal cancer will come back and eventually kill them. It's all I can focus on.

We knew when we got him in 2018 that his time was already limited. He was ten, almost eleven, when he came home with us and we took him full well knowing this. We had hoped he would be ours forever. However, with the news from the Vet, I realized in an instant, that forever isn't long enough. Now time means something different. Now time was an enemy, ticking down. Now time would be the one thing we wanted, but couldn't have and there was no way to get more

The Vet and I talk and while I don't have to decide right now, we both know that his options are limited and he is facing death. Not maybe, not a miracle, but his end in no uncertain terms.

Shattered is the only word that comes to mind. I drive home lost in my thoughts and perhaps the short distance from the Vet to our house is good in this sense.

Life also has a way of saying: "You need a bit more on your plate? Here you go!" Turns out that when I get home my wife isn't feeling too good. She waves it off as nothing, but sure enough, she tests positive for Covid. There is no way to plan life. Two major events in one day. For the moment, I have to compartmentalize Gunner's prognosis and focus on taking care of my wife.

DETERMINED TO MAKE TIME MATTER

2-5-22

GUNNER THE BEAGLE HERE!

It's been really busy around here. The lady hooman isn't feeling well. She has to stay upstairs. Sometimes I stay with her during the day while she is in bed. She says I make her feel better!

My hooman seems to be doing better, he's not crying anymore. He was squeezing me really tight and petting me a lot like something was wrong. He kept telling me it would be okay and singing something about "it's going to be alright." I'm not sure what he means, of course things will be alright, I have you hooman!

But maybe there is something he is not telling me? My sniffer... feels different. It's sort of itchy on one side and doesn't work as good. Maybe if I rub it into the carpet it will go away!

Nope. Still there. I trust my hooman to make it better. Smart hooman, he always knows!

GUNNER'S PERSON HERE

Smart hooman? Always knows? I wish that were true. I wish I was smart as Gunner thinks I am.

We've come to grips with what we are facing and realize we have to be strong for him. All the while being heartbroken and feeling helpless with not being able to fix him. He, of course, doesn't know what he faces and that this will end his life. He just knows something isn't quite right.

I haven't had the opportunity to even catch my breath here. It's been so chaotic with my wife's Covid. I've been shouldering a lot and just trying to keep my head above water and hold the house together has left me drained. My wife is coming out of the toughest part of Covid and is doing better and just now ending quarantine. Life gets a bit back to normal.

As soon as we're (largely) over the hurdle of my wife's illness my mind returns focus to Gunner. I'm not sure of the right word with where I am with Gunner's prognosis. There is the five stages of grief and all, but I'm finding I'm not in any of them. I have accepted it right from the beginning based on what I've read. There is no curing this. There is only delaying it and that is typically in younger dogs. Gunner isn't young.

Armed with the fact that his time is short, I'm determined to make his last months memorable. I've read about "doggy bucket lists" and I shy away from calling it that. Instead it's "Gunner's to do list..." ride in a fire truck, eat steak, learn to speak, you name it. Could be that by calling it something different. I'm trying to not think too much about what is really going on.

In a way this list, is as much for me as it is for him. A way to keep my mind off the cruel inevitable fate that we can't escape.

While we can't know exactly when it will be, we are determined to do as much as we can with the time left and somehow that will have to be enough.

MY FRIEND TIMBER

2-15-22

GUNNER THE BEAGLE HERE!

My friend Timber is not feeling too good today. She couldn't make it inside from all the white stuff outside. My hooman and the boy hooman had to carry her back inside. She can't seem to walk now, I'm scared for her. My hooman puts blankets down in the kitchen and Timber doesn't want to move from them. She seems very tired at the moment.

They are sad and crying. Is something really, really wrong with her? I hope not. She has been my only dog friend since Bandit. I'll lay next to her to keep her company. She likes that and I stay right next to her to keep her safe.

She doesn't really want to move much. She's not drinking her water?

I'm worried about her and my hooman looks really concerned too. I'm sure he'll know what to do.

GUNNER'S PERSON HERE

We thought it would be Gunner first. Turns out it was Timber. She was our second golden and a good girl, but seems to have suffered a stroke where she couldn't walk. She has been on pain medication for a while but it's been tougher for her to get about with no apparent cause. She is not quite ten years old and the blow reminds of us our other Golden, Teddy who was just a bit over eight years old.

Life has a funny way of turning you on your head and reminding you: you don't know what you think you do. It was only a few weeks ago that we got the news about Gunner and here we are with Timber.

Timber is closest to my daughter and she takes it hardest. Timber and Gunner have gotten along well since we brought him home. He seems to know she is not well and lays down next to her during the last hours before we take her to the Vet.

I have been discussing with the Vet some of her symptoms that we have been treating for a while now but this is sudden. She doesn't want to or can't move at all. She has no interest in food or water when we bring it over to her. She seems to know and is looking at us wondering why we are not getting it.

A call to the Vet and we discuss it. We know it's time for her.

We pet her and lay on the floor with her as she can't really move. We sing to her and talk to her in soothing tones and tell her how much we love her. As always, she is happy and smiling and liking the attention. She has been a great girl and ever since she got out of her puppy stage, a gentle, sweet dog.

As we leave the house that feeling hits me again. I haven't had to do this in almost ten years: taking a dog to be euthanized. It's that sinking deep in the pit of one's stomach feeling that what you are about to do, while for the best, means you are going to be without your dog. It's the price we pay for dogs. Their shorter lifespans means any dog lover is going to have to do this, likely multiple times in their lives. We have had her since she was eight months old and she filled the void after Teddy.

My wife and I bring her inside our Vet's office and the process proceeds. She is quickly asleep from the sedative and is very peaceful. More peaceful than she has been in a while. Her pain medication was keeping her comfortable prior, but now she is truly relaxed. The Vet steps away to let us say our final goodbyes and we cry and speak softly to her. I know what I have to do and at the same time I don't want to do it, I can't drag it out any longer and call for the Vet to come back in.

Timber never shutters or makes a sound she simply stops breathing. We stay with her for quite a bit, not wanting to leave her. Knowing that this is the last time we'll see her is tough. Finally, we can't do it anymore and leave sobbing.

It hits hard because we loved her, and also know that in the not too distant future, we are going to have to do this again with Gunner.

On the way home we have one thought, run golden girl and be pain free, the Rainbow Bridge is waiting for you and Sammy and Teddy will be there waiting to meet you.

SPEAK, MY PERSON SAYS?

2-17-22

GUNNER THE BEAGLE HERE!

My hooman keeps saying "speak", "speak." He's waving around treats when he says it too. Huh? I don't get it. I'm speaking right now, can't you understand me hooman? What's wrong with you, you're usually much smarter than this!

Wait, oh I get it. He wants me to do that thing I'm not supposed to do, okay hooman, you asked for it!

(Beagle bark/howl), Aryoo!!!

I'm a good boy for speaking! I have a great voice, right hoomans?

REFLECTIONS

FAVORITE 2-22-22

I made the decision that on my birthday I wanted to do something for Gunner. With that in mind I took him to visit my brother who is a fireman at the local airport (now since retired). This photo was not long after he got his diagnosis and perhaps my favorite photo of the two of us.

TOGETHER 3-20-22

One of my wife's favorite photos of the two of us. It really encapsulates his demeanor in my opinion. There were no treats in the offing here, just me picking him up for a photo. I'm ever so glad we have this photo of him.

EASTER BEAGLE 4-17-22

Our old boy was great about this. Even when he got sick he was as gentle as could be and would tolerate the ears and bandannas. I think he knew treats came next!

CAR RIDE 5-23-22

Normally rides in vehicles were just Gunner and I. This time out my wife was driving and my daughter photographing from the back seat. We got a number of photos where his smile was caught in the side mirror, but liked this one best of all.

BITTERSWEET 5-28-22

This is another favorite of mine. This is on the day I took Gunner for one last visit to the shelter where he was rescued and where he became our dog. He's still happy, but his tumor is starting to get worse here. It's a great photo, but bittersweet.

BEAGLE SCOUT 6-19-22

Still very much with it and happy, he eagerly posed for his "Beagle Scout" photos. Here is our old boy being a good sport as always and munching on treats.

MIXED FEELINGS 7-21-22

I struggled whether or not put this photo in. By now he was very sick and over the last two weeks of his life, his cancer spread and his face swelled. Looking back on it I'm conflicted. Up until late June, early July the tumor was manageable, but right after the 4th of July it became very aggressive and swelled. He was alert and with it up to his last day.

GUNNER'S PERSON HERE

When we first got Gunner we remarked that for a beagle just how quiet he was. I often wondered if it was due to his previous life. I suspect that he learned early on that no matter how much he whined, cried or howled, it wasn't going to matter. This is only a guess, as I can't know his previous life for sure, but I think it's a good guess. If true, to me that is also a cruel thing to do. Dogs are pack animals, they want to be part of the pack. So I decided to help him learn to bark as part of his doggy to do list before...well... before he passes...

Knowing his food driven nature, I coaxed his bark from him with treats and sure enough he realized he had a voice.

He seems rather pleased with himself through the whole thing and picks it up quickly, so much for the saying that "you can't teach an old dog new tricks." There is also the possibility he is only doing it because there is food involved. The flip side is very quickly he has learned what it means and will do it even if I'm not waving a dog treat around.

No matter the result, it is heartwarming to hear a beagle bark from a beagle who perhaps never realized he had one. I helped him find his actual voice, one that he always had, but perhaps forgot somewhere along the way.

I may have helped but Gunner did the work. All credit to him for speaking.

LAZY SATURDAY MORNING

2-19-22

GUNNER THE BEAGLE HERE!

I'm a bit snuffly this morning. There is a small lump on my snout that makes me wheezy sometimes, but the pills my hooman gives me makes it feel better. I like these pills things. They taste okay I guess. Sometimes I catch my hooman hiding them in stuff, doesn't he know I can smell it? Silly hooman!

Today however is a lazy morning with my hooman watching the snow fall from the front windows. I like it much better in here warm and cozy snuggled next to my hooman. He's warm, just like Bandit but even warmer! I think I'll just cozy in here and go back to sleep. ZZZ...

GUNNER'S PERSON HERE

The last few days he's been sounding stuffy so I'm monitoring him. When he's at rest he's generally alright with his breathing. His tumor is noticeable but at bay for the moment. I'm really starting from scratch here as we don't know how fast or slow this will grow.

Today we we spent an hour or so just laying on the fold-out bed in the living room. I opened up the curtains and we just looked at the snow for a while on a lazy winter day. More like it was me looking at the snow while I gently pet him and he snoozed. Gunner is sometimes weird with touch, but on this day he's happy to snuggle next to me, absorb warmth, and let me gently pet him.

It's days like this that having a dog is close to perfect, but as we recently affirmed, with having to put down Timber, I know days like this won't last forever. My mind wanders to Timber. We haven't even caught our breath from the finality of Timber. The end was so sudden that it caught us off guard. Timber was such a complex dog for me in terms of my emotions. Part of it was we literally got her days after having to put down Teddy and it was such a blur that it clouded my interactions with her. I loved her and took care of her as best as I could, but I just can't put into words what I felt with her.

Of course, I then start thinking about Gunner and what this is going to be like. There is no road map but I am keenly aware of time. Gunner has a finite amount of time. He isn't going to get anymore. I suppose that is true about all of us. At the same time, for many of us, we don't know exactly when that will be. True, I don't know exactly when for Gunner either, but I do know that there is no escaping his cancer.

FIRE TRUCK RIDE!

2-22-22

GUNNER THE BEAGLE HERE!

Today I didn't do too much because I knew I was going to have fun this evening! My hooman told me so. My hooman is smart I tell him all the time, maybe I get more treats that way? I wonder where we are going. I hope it's not another one of the trips to get a bath! I like the way I smell!

The lady hooman keeps saying something about "you're getting old" and looking at my hooman! Hah, hear that hooman, you're old, not me!

Late today my hoomans took me on a trip to the airport fire department where I got to pose with my hooman and hooman's brother! I even got to ride in a fire truck! It is big and my hooman has to hoist me up and into the truck ("oof"), I'm not scared though. I'm very brave! It was a big surprise for me!

We got to drive around too. It was fun to be up there. Does that make me a fire dog now? Forget those spotted dogs! Gunner the fire dog here! I help put out fires by going wee-wee on things. Speaking of which, I have to go now. Let me out of this thing!

Who knew a fire truck ride could be so much fun?

GUNNER'S PERSON HERE

Normally I try to do a selfless act on my birthday, like give blood and encourage others to do so. Sure, I hope for good karma from it so perhaps not entirely unselfish. But today I wanted to do something for Gunner because I know that likely by the next birthday I won't have him…so perhaps for me as well, as this is about saying goodbye in a way that we couldn't for our other dogs.

At this stage of my life, I don't need anything for my birthday. All I need is Gunner and that is the one thing that is in a finite supply. We often worry about things or presents, material wants but in the end, I've come to realize that having a pet who is so strongly bonded to me is a far greater gift than I can ever imagine.

We brought him to the airport fire department and he got to ride on a truck and pose with my brother and I. We have him wearing a yellow bandanna to match the color of the truck he is riding on. It's part of the list of all the things I want to do with him before he passes, and since he likes to ride in trucks, a fire truck should be even better, right? He likes the ride in the fire truck very much and is happy to wander around and sniff stuff and meet the other fire fighters afterwards. Of course he has to go outside to do his business, all part of having to make the place his.

He seemed to enjoy himself and like he always does, made the place his own.

He's happy to be the center of attention (while he's not trying to get into the garbage). I'm happy also. But more so, I'm happy that he is happy. I can't imagine my birthday being any better. I don't need any birthday presents. I have Gunner. And looking at the photos we take, the smile on his face is huge. I didn't notice while we were there but it's as big of a grin as I've ever seen on his face.

CHEESEBURGER, OH YEAH...
2-26-22

GUNNER THE BEAGLE HERE!

It's been a few days and I'm ready for my close up my hooman says? What the heck does that mean hooman? He has that phone thing out again and the other hooman is taking pictures. Wait does this mean I have to wear antlers again? Oh just pictures? Okay I guess just make sure you get my good side away from the lump.

Wait what is the hooman unwrapping? The other hooman says "it's your burger buddy!" I sniff it and it smells really good, hey wait, give me that! NOM NOM NOM!

What's that (crunch) you're recording me on (bite) those phone things? Don't care, this is good!

I'm finished! Can I have another one?

GUNNER'S PERSON HERE

Part of the list: one cheeseburger.

I made sure it didn't have any onions as I know dogs aren't supposed to have those...but at this stage, however, it's really not a concern now. We desperately want him to be around as long as possible, but we wanted to check this one off the list. Knowing all this, we settle on a simple cheeseburger and he as he always does, takes the food gently and eats the bun first which we found amusing.

In a way, we are always amazed that while he is so hungry for food, even now, that he is always very meek about taking it from the hand. No aggression or "wolfing it down." You'd never know he hadn't had one before. Maybe he has? It occurs to me as I watch him eating it for all we know cheeseburgers are all he ever ate.

It brings me back to the day we brought him home, looking at him thinking how many unknowns there are with a dog, particularly one of his age: almost eleven at the time. With a puppy, a person is able to share all their experiences from very beginning, not so with Gunner.

Snapping back to the present, it's a marvel how one's mind can leap from the simple act of watching your dog eat to thinking about all the other things he's likely experienced that you have no idea about.

All I do know on this day is he's happy and well loved. Not sure he cares about any of that, he's happy and he's eating a cheeseburger. For dogs, it sometimes is that simple: just eating food and being happy. That's a great lesson.

BONES AND SUCH

2-28-22

 ## GUNNER THE BEAGLE HERE!

Something about "my food adventures continue?" Today my hoomans gave me peanut butter inside my bone! NOM NOM NOM! Way to go hoomans, you do my bidding! Wait a minute, this looks like my old bone, you just put more peanut butter in it! I don't care what they did, it's good!

Timber isn't here to eat hers. Maybe the hoomans will put peanut butter in that one two. I'll take care of it for her. I miss my friend Timber. I miss she is gone. The hoomans say she is with the other dogs now: Sammy and Teddy.

Can I go meet them too and play?

GUNNER'S PERSON HERE

Throughout the years, we have given the dogs marrow bones and it will usually keep them busy for hours. Out of all of them Gunner is the most relentless on the bones. He'll go until he gets all the marrow out and then some. Once done, we load up with the peanut butter which he loves.

I'm finding that in the days after Timber's passing, while not searching for her per se, there is something "off" about him and I don't think it can be explained away by the tumor itself. He looks to have acknowledged she is gone, but isn't seeking her out or the stories of some dogs being distraught when their dog friend is no longer around.

The simple activity of filling his bone and letting him work it over is comforting for all of us. We watch him and he barely pays us any mind, his sole focus is on that bone, nothing else exists in his world. In a lot of ways I envy him. I wish I could forget about my troubles and cares, and to forget Gunner's diagnosis, if only for a while to quiet my mind.

Bones were big for Timber too. For a long while before Gunner, she was our only dog. She would always take them from us so gingerly and find a spot. Unusually the only time we ever saw her get somewhat protective of food were bones. Not growl but more of a side eye indicating "You're trying to do what now with my bone?"

We're all sad with Timber's sudden passing and in the end stages of winter, it sometimes makes for some bleak thoughts to match the dreary weather. We realize that once the weather breaks and it's time to recommence walks, that it will be with only one dog, not two. Maybe that has been something we have all blocked out, maybe it's something we haven't even considered until now.

In my pondering I stop and pause: in the space of a few moments I've leapt from bones, peanut butter, weather to walks. It's crazy to think of how solely caring for Gunner is now wrapped up in a lot of different things and emotions.

SNOUT AND WHITE STUFF!

3-1-22

GUNNER THE BEAGLE HERE!

It's getting somewhat warmer now. The white stuff on the ground is starting to get patchy. That means it's going to get warmer soon! I like it when the white stuff goes away, warmer is better.

My snout is still really itchy. My hooman gives me extra stuff for it and it feels a little better.

But I finally found a use for the white stuff! Sometimes I stick my whole face in the white stuff when I go outside to go wee-wee. Other times I like to rub my face around in it. The lump seems to feel better when its cold. I don't like this lump...It hurts sometimes.

Maybe the hooman can take me to that place and fix it like they did my eye!

GUNNER'S PERSON HERE

Winter is in its last stages, but there is a lot of snow. I suspect he has gotten over his dislike of it knowing that it feels good on his face. I wish I could do more to take his pain away. He's doing this a lot lately as I suspect it feels good for him.

Gunner is on his medication for pain, but he's also really, really leaning in for his ears to be scratched. Sometimes I dig inside them which he really likes…ugh. I also have to be mindful that the tumor is likely growing and it feels good, but I have to be careful. This can't be easy for him.

Throughout this I've become more mindful of his journey. I think about when I had to do this for my father who had a stroke. One salient point comes back to me: it's not about what I want, it's about what my father wants. This isn't about what I want, it's about what is best for Gunner.

Of course in this case, Gunner can't make decisions on his own. I can't know what he wants because as a dog he's likely not even aware of what he is facing on the level that a human understands. That makes it even harder. I have to think for him. I am responsible for him of course, that's what you sign up for when you get a dog. I'm finding the decision of life and death isn't one I want, nor would anyone when it comes to their dog. We couch it in euphemisms of "best interest" or "doing what is right by them" or something else. At its most fundamental level though, when you strip everything away, it's the same as making life and death decisions for a family member.

I just had to do it for my father right before Gunner came home. Facing it again, no matter the rationalization, isn't something I want to do, but have to regardless. Again I come back to this isn't what I want, it is what is "best" for Gunner. If it was, he would live forever with me. Life doesn't work that way.

RESTLESS AT NIGHT

3-5-22

GUNNER THE BEAGLE HERE!

Last night was rough. It took me almost a thing the hoomans call an hour before I could settle down next to my person for bed! I have no idea what an hour is, but it did seem long. He let me outside then in, back out again. I needed water, but then I didn't really want it. Then I had to go back outside again!

I'm not really sure why...usually I can fall asleep easy. I'm really good at sleeping! My snout was itchy again. I can't seem to shake it off. Sniffer not working right again too. That lump is making it hard to see, and sleep too? What the heck is this lump thing? I want it gone pronto!

Through it all though? My hooman did my bidding! Yes hooman, you do what I want! You are my hooman and a good one. I think I'll keep you around!

Oh and by morning? I had most of the bed and was pushing him off the side! I have no idea what that means other than my hooman was grumbling about "move over Gunner!"

Hah! This is my bed silly hooman. You are just here to be my heater!

ZZZ...

GUNNER'S PERSON HERE

Last night was tough. He was really congested and would not settle down. I wondered if this was the start of "it" as it were, but eventually with a lot of inside and outside, water, and petting him, I got him to calm down. There were some points that were actually quite concerning. Was he going to pass away right there with me at 3 AM? I have been preparing myself to be parted from him, but not this suddenly.

He seemed out of sorts for a lot of the night, almost as if he knew something was wrong, but not knowing exactly what. I wouldn't say he was confused, rather it was like he didn't quite know what was going on.

One part that is toughest on us: we don't know if it's three months, is it five, or is it less? The Vet gave us a range. There is no way to know this and we can only go by her guidance and what we have read up on the subject.

Another conflicting part of this is knowing each day what this disease is doing to him and at the same time, trying to put it out of our minds. The anguish of this dual reality is near impossible to rationalize. At this stage, he is in good health for the most part, but slowly creeping towards his ultimate demise. I can't think of any other way to frame it because we know how this ends.

Have to take each day as it comes. It's all we can do and hope and pray that we keep him as comfortable and pain free as we possibly can for as long as we can.

WINDY DAY!

3-7-22

🐾 GUNNER THE BEAGLE HERE!

I took my hoomans for a walk today! Good hoomans! I haven't gone on one of those for quite a while!

Only problem was the wind! I almost flew away! My floppy ears were flopping all around. It did feel good to get air in them. Sometimes the hooman digs around there too, that feels really good when he does that! Sometimes I make low happy noises to tell him how much I love it!

Oh yeah the wind! Doesn't matter, I went on a walk as all the white stuff melted!

I got really scared when the winds got bad. I remember when I was outside with Bandit and we only had each other, it was scary! But my hooman picked me up ("oof") and carried me home. Good hooman, he always knows.

GUNNER'S PERSON HERE

Weather around here is like that. We get all four seasons and Spring as of late has at least one wind event. We tried getting out before the winds got really bad as it was nice, temperature showed 70. It hasn't been that temperature in months. The problem was the winds also got to 70 mph gusts. When we started, the wind storm was a ways away, but it moved up quickly.

We eventually had to stop as it was too much for him. He was ready to fly away. No joke. The winds were pushing him around and his ears all over the place. One of the neighbors trampolines dislodged from its moorings, went sailing across the street, and smashed the front of a car. That's how windy it got (happened on our way back).

When the winds subsided between gusts, he would continue on the walk. I have a feeling though that those ten years living outside prior to us taught him to "hunker down" as it were. The walk today didn't really tell us too much of how up he is for walks since his diagnosis. We had to put them on hold over the winter for Timber and for him being so low to the ground and congested.

Through March the weather will moderate. It won't be warm for several more months, but it should be warm enough to get him out for small walks. Trouble is summer here gets very humid and by June daytime temperatures can get high. We'll have to deal with it then and if he is still going on walks three months from now. I'll count that as no small thing and not bat an eye at the temperatures as long as he can tolerate it.

MY BIRTHDAY TODAY

3-14-22

GUNNER THE BEAGLE HERE!

My hoomans say I'm 14, not sure what that means because I'm 98 in my years! Of course I'm not sure what a year is either… remember? I can't count, one, two, lots!

The cake my hoomans made for me was the best! Good hoomans! They sang a song me, all four of them and my hooman picked me up ("oof") and held me while they sang. There was a lot of smoke. I hope the loud beeping doesn't start up again! I hate that loud beeping!

Wait a minute! When these things happen they usually put something on my head and make me look all funny...I don't see anything around. Maybe they are hiding it on me and will put it on later? Sneaky hoomans!

It's all over, they are done singing? Give me the cake now! Yum this is good! I want to eat the whole thing. The other hooman says its "all for you." I don't have to share any of this?

GUNNER'S PERSON HERE

Today we celebrated his first mini milestone since getting the bad news in January. Once we got over the initial shock, we wanted to get him to his birthday today. Bittersweet and perhaps very fortunate as had his birthday been in December; I don't think he has that much time. I hope I'm wrong and at the same time, deep down, I know I'm not. His birthday was at least in the back of my mind, somber, and quiet because we know that this is his last.

He very much liked his cake. My wife did a great job with it and the candles, me holding him and us blowing out the candles all caught on video. He seemed a bit perplexed during the process, but liked the end result of getting the cake.

Time, however, is rearing its ugly head. Even in happy moments like this, reminding us that the sands of time are running out. While time may be short, he's doing good so far. Here's hoping I'm still wondering just when he will take a turn for the worse a year from now. I know that won't be the case, but hope is what keeps me going sometimes. We've lost Timber and it's looming with Gunner. Not easy at all.

Pushing that aside and focusing though, today was a good day. Our old boy made it to his birthday and that's the big thing. Everything else from here on out is a gift. Our next goal is for him to make it to Easter and the weather being good enough to perhaps take him to some parks.

That right now looks to be the best way to approach this: a series of small goals and take each one as it comes and then look to the next. It has the benefit of also distracting us from the end. It's something I'm keenly aware of but one I can't dwell on now.

FALSE HOPE

4-6-22

GUNNER THE BEAGLE HERE!

My...my lump seems to be shrinking?!? That is a good thing. My hooman seems to be happy about it. I just like that my sniffer seems to be working better. Either way, I'm feeling good!

My hoomans say they have an "Easter surprise" for me... what the heck is an Easter surprise? That's usually not good as I get dressed up goofy when there are "surprises." Better not be the antlers again I'm watching you hoomans!

The white stuff is gone from the ground. That means that the warm days are ahead! I like it when the white stuff leaves. It means soon I can lay outside and warm up like I always do!

I like being warm.

GUNNER'S PERSON HERE

It does indeed look like his tumor has gotten smaller. He seems to be doing well, happy, and chugging along. We've been getting him out for walks as long as the weather has allowed since it's been unusually cold here; way below normal temps.

The tumor, or the lump as we call it, does indeed seem to be smaller as of late. It's stayed largely the same size for the last month and then about a week ago, we noticed it had reduced in size. It's not bothering him at the moment. He does occasionally paw at it and is on some mild pain medication for any discomfort. As of right now, there are no other symptoms.

We know this is likely just a brief respite as there is no curing his cancer. I keep thinking and calling it false hope because I'm torn with the idea of hope in general right now. I know we need it, but understand the finality of what is coming. That is what is making what we are seeing with him right now so frustrating: we should be happy, but can't allow ourselves based on what we know.

At least at this point in the process, it gives us a moment to pause. The Vet told us three to four months. It's rapidly coming up to the lower end of that estimate. We have to be brave for him. Brave in this situation isn't an absence of fear as we know what awaits. Rather, it's being brave in spite of the fear.

Fortunately for us, Gunner continues to be himself. When we first got him, I described him as meek and mild. In some ways he is still that. But the other day my wife was at work and the kids were asleep when I got up. After eating and doing his business outside, he followed me upstairs and we simply played on the floor. He rolled on his back, pawed at me, made noises, and had a grand time. It warmed my heart that here was this old dog, facing certain death, and not knowing it, and playing like a puppy. Whatever sins or faults I have in my life, which are likely many, I at least have this gift of a beautiful dog. And in that I am thankful beyond measure.

EASTER BEAGLE?

4-17-22

GUNNER THE BEAGLE HERE!

My hoomans say today is Easter. I have no idea what that is. All I know is I'm wearing ears bigger than my actual ones…I get treats for this? Wait is this that "surprise" they were talking about? You did this to me a while back too with the antlers! How come I keep falling for this? I should know better by now!

You better not have any more surprises. I'm wise to you hooman! These "holiday things" seem to be an excuse to dress me up. Better not be putting me in my "everything bagel" t-shirt again! Hope I didn't just give him ideas…

Alright I'll tolerate the bunny ears just this once as the lady hooman says I "look really cute!" Well of course I do lady, I'm Gunner, I look cute every day, duh!

The girl hooman has her phone thingy out and is taking lots of pictures and says she'll send them to my hooman. He's grinning now too about posting them? I have no idea what a post is. Oh wait, you mean for me to go wee-wee on it? I like those posts!

Anyways where were we?

Treats now?

GUNNER'S PERSON HERE

The old guy is a good sport with these types of things. I found some bunny ears, the headband kind kids wear and placed them on him. Like at Christmas with the reindeer antlers, he seems not to mind or at least not be too bothered with them. I suspect it's because he knows treats are in the offing.

More importantly, Gunner reached our goal of getting to Easter. When we found out his prognosis in January, it seemed impossible for him to make it this far. First was making sure he got to his birthday in March, then to Easter. Looking ahead is getting tougher. Maybe Memorial Day, on the outside 4th of July?

Despite him getting to this point, he's back to be being congested again. The tumor while still there, hasn't gotten any smaller than it was. It also hasn't gotten any bigger either. All we can do now is keep hoping against hope.

Weather is still not cooperating for some small hikes and photo shoots, but I take comfort in the fact we've already done a lot on his doggy list. I'm going to have to come up with more. Even if I don't, the time spent with him has to be enough. There is no other way for me to look at it that makes sense without an overwhelming sense of too many emotions.

Lastly on this particular Easter, I try to focus on (relatively speaking) things are about as best as we can hope for right now. The Vet said back in January that with his prognosis he had three to four months (maybe) to live. We know we're already beating the odds with him. It should help, but it doesn't.

UNHAPPY WITH MY HOOMAN!

5-14-22

GUNNER THE BEAGLE HERE!

My hooman was busy all day! I'm not happy. He was neglecting me. I keep telling the small hoomans I need my hooman, but they are clueless as usual! I WANT MY HOOMAN! I've never been so unhappy with him! How dare he leave me!

Maybe if I go to the door and whine and cry someone will take pity on me and let me out! Better yet, I'll make a break for it and show him! Maybe the whine and cry routine will work? No, the lady hooman isn't here, she always falls for that!

Finally he comes inside! What's this he needs a shower then will "head outside?" I better watch him to make sure. In fact, I'm going to sit right outside that shower thing to make sure he isn't trying to pull something when I'm not looking.

HE DID IT! HE LET ME OUT! I'm going outside with the hoomans now!

He did bring out a blanket for me as a peace offering. What, no steak? I'm wise to his game and I'm still mad, so I'm laying on the flat stones outside the front of the house to show him! Better sleep with one eye open just to make sure...

ZZZ...

GUNNER'S PERSON HERE

Crying and crying today that I was NOT RIGHT NEXT TO HIM due to yard work. Looking back on it, as I sit here, a sense of guilt comes over me. The lawn could have waited, time with him can't be replaced.

Despite it being reported by my kids that he was indeed out of sorts while I was outside, he does settle down and sleep on the driveway once we sit down to relax. The weather is warm and I think he likes the heat from the driveway.

He's now on stronger medication for pain. I don't think he's too bad at this point, but the tumor site is sore for him. His poor sniffer is really dry now. He still has his appetite and is drinking well so all is good as can be. He's happy just to be near us.

The timeline the Vet gave us in late January was he only had three to four months left to live. We're now approaching the end of that. At the same time because of that I'm thankful for each day. It's an important reminder to make each day count.

I make a mental note to be aware of these types of days because soon they will be gone. Will I regret the fact that I didn't mow the lawn or will I regret fact that I didn't spend more time with Gunner? I'm of the opinion that regret is one of the most useless emotions: the past can't be changed so why waste time and energy over it? When it comes to Gunner, however, emotion overwhelms my logic.

TO ENDURE WHAT IS TO COME

5-22-22

GUNNER THE BEAGLE HERE!

I'm a bit sore and my snout is not good, but I have my hoomans to stay by my side no matter what! I'm getting to eat whatever I want these days too! Aryooo!!!!

The lump...is getting bigger, it's getting harder for me to see out my right eye.

My hooman seems sad today. I'll go lay next to him and cheer him up. Oh good it's working, he isn't as sad now and is petting me. Maybe if I roll over he can scratch my belly and that will do the trick.

I get treats for this?

GUNNER'S PERSON HERE

Today is a tougher day…we know we are getting closer to the end. His snout is sore and has not reduced in swelling and a few other symptoms I don't want to share. His pain medication is keeping him comfortable. He's okay as of now, but in a week a lot of things can change.

We're on a roller coaster of emotions. This is uncharted territory for all of us. All of our previous dogs have been sudden or for sudden reasons. Gunner's illness is protracted and we are handling it as best as we can. Various songs come to mind and drill home how I can't fix my buddy and can only ease his pain. This will be the fourth time I've had to put a dog down and this is going to be the hardest, harder than Teddy. Teddy and Timber were sudden, with Gunner we've known it's coming.

KNOWING ALL WE CAN DO IS HOPE AND KEEP HIM COMFORTABLE

We don't have much time and what I've been dreading is getting closer. What that time frame looks like I don't know, but I don't want him to suffer. When we first got him, I was of the mindset of "whatever time we have with him for will be enough." Now it doesn't seem like enough. Not by a long shot.

I keep coming back to a movie, and a scene that is somewhat maudlin, with one of the characters stating:

"It is always ready to excuse, to trust, to hope, and to endure… whatever comes." That pause is where I'm existing now. Knowing all we can do is endure. Knowing that despite what is coming there is nothing else more important than to bear the unbearable. Knowing all we can do is hope and keep him comfortable. The "it" is love. It's love that wants to keep him by my side, now and forever. It's also that same love that means soon I'll have to be parted from him.

I tell everyone who will listen, pet your dogs, take them for that walk even when you don't want to. They will make messes, have accidents. It all seems so small now. We are their whole world, we owe it to them. Dogs, and in particular, my Gunner, are perfect, imperfect creatures and ones we are sometimes unworthy of to have in our lives.

SIGNS ARE APPEARING

5-27-22

GUNNER THE BEAGLE HERE!

The other day when my hooman made me pose for photos. Does he know who I am? I'm a star! Give up the food and treats while you're at it hooman!

I've been posing in these silly bandannas for months and now you want to take some photos of me in them? What gives here? I better be getting some treats for this! Did you hear that? TREATS!

Ooooh...what is this? Chicken? Okay I'll be good, just how many photos are we talking and make it fast!

We're done? Let me at it!

GUNNER'S PERSON HERE

His appetite is slowing on most days. Could be because of him getting more selective for food too. As a result, today we make him chicken which makes him very happy. Almost as if he knew that posing for photos meant he was going to get something special. As a breed, beagles are very single minded given their purpose as hunting dogs and sometimes accounted as stubborn or not easy to train. This is made up for their pliant nature and in the case of Gunner, very much understanding the concept of actions equals food reward.

On the health front, his symptoms of the past few days are subsiding and his current pain medication seems to be doing the job. The Vet and I have been talking and we are preparing next steps if he starts showing signs of discomfort.

He still loves his walks, but they seem to be bit more tiring for him. So we cut them short as needed. He gives us signs and it is up to us to be aware of them and adjust accordingly.

As we return home, my mind wanders to the senior citizen status of our beagle. Had he been a young beagle he would have never been surrendered in the first place. As a puppy, it would have really, really never happened. Senior dogs face this all too often.

For a variety of reasons people do not usually consider senior dogs when adopting. They require more care. They will pass away sooner. But having gone on this journey and looking back on his journey with us, we keep coming back to: if we didn't adopt Gunner no one would have. He would have ended out his days at the shelter. I don't say that to applaud our own efforts; Gunner has given us far more in return than we could have ever hoped for. But the fact remains that senior dogs are sometimes the most difficult to get adopted out.

I never thought I'd adopt a senior dog myself for many of the same reasons I just listed. A former coworker of mind did this all the time and I thought she was crazy for doing so.

Now I get it.

And taking that all in, I understand just how much poorer and the void that there would be in my life had Gunner not entered and filled it. That is worth the approaching pain and one I'm willing to bear. I owe him that.

A LAST REUNION

5-28-22

GUNNER THE BEAGLE HERE!

Truck ride with my hooman today, he didn't tell me where we were going, but I love truck rides!

As always, my hooman lifts me into the truck ("oof") and I cozy into my spot and I ride off with my person! I secretly like it when he does that. I feel safe with him when just the two of us go on rides together. It's one of my favorite things.

It's warm out now and the window things are down. I'm too old to stick my head out the window so I slept most of the way.

When I wake up I'm at a familiar place, my hooman says "we're here." We are back at the shelter? I remember this place and I get scared and look at my hooman; he says we are "just visiting." That's good, I'm too old to go back.

Inside are the nice shelter ladies...I remember them! We stay for quite a while. The hoomans talk and some smaller hoomans pet me and give me treats. It was a long time ago that I was here, I think. The shelter ladies are very nice and happy to see me.

For a long time I thought this was going to be my home until my hoomans came and got me.

GUNNER'S PERSON HERE

It was a fine morning for a drive, just the two of us. As we have almost always done we ride in silence, no radio, no nothing just me occasionally petting him.

This morning has a purpose to the drive as I'm taking him to visit with some of the volunteers at the shelter where we got him. In particular, one I've kept in touch with in the years since he came home.

As usual Gunner liked his truck ride and snuggled into his blanket on the seat.

When we got out he recognized the place and eagerly went around like he had never left. Inside we visit with the shelter staff and some of the younger volunteers who pet Gunner and he was fine with attention. We talk and laugh about all the great things about Gunner. We posed for photos and he smiled a big grin like the photo that drew us to him a few years before. During the conversations he wanders around the offices sniffing. Again I was struck by how he remembered the place and it wasn't from the smell or maybe it was.

Towards the end, we reminisce about the day he came home and all around it's happy. Gunner and I say our goodbyes and head off from this last reunion with the shelter, I know its likely to be the last.

On the ride home I don't really say much, but just pet him. Like he always does every once in a while, he opens an eye to make sure I'm still there. I told you before buddy, I'm here and always will be.

At one point on the way home the finality of it hits me, so much closer to the end than the beginning. I silently weep as I drive, glancing over at my dog. I love him more than anything and the sadness is overwhelming.

PREENING FOR MY FANS!

6-5-22

GUNNER THE BEAGLE HERE!

What gives? My hoomans took me for my walk early??? What the heck a morning walk? Don't they know my fan base isn't out for me to preen for? Seriously, all those people I need to visit (and mark in their yards), trucks to try and climb in??? I'm a star!

Do my bidding hoomans! I demand my closeup! But my non-lump side while you're at it…Wait where is everyone, they should be coming out of their houses right now to marvel at me! No they aren't coming outside to see me, well then, let's turn around!

The hoomans aren't turning around? I guess I'll just have to wee-wee on more stuff than usual as we go around. And sniff more stuff too. And stop and stare. Maybe they will get it; probably not, silly hoomans.

GUNNER'S PERSON HERE

We often remarked about how he HAS to visit everyone on walks and try to get into vehicles, especially trucks. Over the years, he has enjoyed his truck rides with me but I'm fairly confident that it must be some part of his former life he remembers. Then, of course, it could be nothing more than I drive a truck and that's what he associates with me. The bits and pieces of his former life have ever been a mystery to us and we are often left to wonder. It's fine though in this instance, it's just part of what makes Gunner, Gunner.

In terms of walks when he wants to stop, he does just that. Quits walking and starts to scratch at his collar with this weird grin as he does so. In other words, he's preening to some degree. We're not sure how many walks he had prior to us. When we first got him, both he and Timber would just pad along. He learned a lot from her in that way. But over time he developed this trait. Since her passing it has become magnified.

We complete the walk but not after stopping at least ten times to complete this ritual, and mostly with no one around for him to impress. We get the distinct feeling he wasn't all too happy with us going out so early.

Health wise, as of today, he's doing all right. He is not in any obvious signs of pain or discomfort and is on the same level of pain medication. Last night he let me inspect the tumor. It's about what I expected and has likely spread to a few other spots. It has grown a bit more since April and is more solid.

His eating the last few days has been good and this week got a lot of turkey sausage. Water intake likewise good. He is fine mentally and is his normal self, sleeping more to be sure, but in all ways simply Gunner.

BEAGLE SCOUT GUNNER REPORTING!

6-19-22

GUNNER THE BEAGLE HERE!

I've obtained Scouting's highest rank, the Beagle Scout. My hooman says so as he's a Scoutmaster. Don't ask me what that means, all I know is he gave me treats! I hope there aren't too many things I need to do as a Beagle Scout; it's getting harder for me to do stuff these days.

He put this nice, different bandanna on me and the boy hooman and my hooman gave me something called a salute? I have no idea what the salute means, but they we're smiling so I'm happy. Their bandannas are the same as this one? Maybe this means I'm in some sort of club? I've never been in a club before.

After the excitement I wanted to sleep. It's harder for me to breath and I'm very sleepy these days. My hoomans are doing a great job though watching out for me. I'll keep my hoomans.

GUNNER'S PERSON HERE

I have indeed promoted Gunner to the full rank of Beagle Scout. He didn't want any palm clusters on his emblem, treats instead. Not surprising given Gunner.

We bought a lot of different bandannas and he has been wearing them off and on for months but he seemed bothered by them so I stopped. Interestingly, with the Scout neckerchief he didn't seem to mind.

In all seriousness, I can't take credit for this one. We saw treats at a local store and the type were called Beagle Scout and it all clicked. My son has just finished scouting and I have been the Scoutmaster of the Troop. What better way to honor Gunner than to "promote" him to Scouting's highest rank.

One of the points of the Scout Law is to be brave. Gunner, whether he knows it or not, has been very brave in the face of his cancer. He goes about each day as he always does and it gives me strength. Being brave is sometimes about the simple things despite knowing the inevitable and seeing it through to the end. Obviously he doesn't know what awaits, maybe he does, but I can only hope that I live up to that part of the Scout oath when the time comes.

Considering for another moment I dwell on all the points of

the Scout Law: "A scout is Trustworthy, Loyal, Helpful, Friendly, Courteous, Kind, Obedient, Cheerful, Thrifty, Brave, Clean, and Reverent." Like a lot of things as of late, I am considering this when applied to a dog. I'm struck by just how many of them could be applied to a dog. Helpful, Friendly, Kind? That is the essence of a dog's nature.

Maybe it was only to add something to his doggy list of things to do, awarding him the rank. But when I looked at it deeper, like listening to songs differently as of late, dogs can be injected into meaning where they might not otherwise.

This is another reminder of how I'm learning more from him on this journey. I'm thankful that I'm learning, not that I'm on it with him. Conflicted and not even bittersweet, more like wronged. More so for Gunner than anyone else.

RESTLESS AGAIN
6-27-22

GUNNER THE BEAGLE HERE!

Been very sleepy lately except the other night when I kept my hooman up from midnight to 5:00 a.m. I was so unsettled, but he kept me company. My nose is really sore and hurts. He cleaned it up for me and some red stuff was there. He looked really concerned.

I finally fell asleep right next to my hooman and slept a long while. Plus I got ice cream the other day too which was nice. It was a good day, good hooman, I think I'll keep you.

GUNNER'S PERSON HERE

This time it's me with the ZZZ…

Saturday evening into Sunday morning was rough. Sleep was not going to be an option as I knew I had to stay up with him. He finally settled in and fell asleep around 5:30 a.m. He could not get comfortable it seemed, but eventually settled in and slept.

In terms of health, he's doing as best as can be expected. He had his first bloody nose and has been something I've been on the lookout for. The cancer is in his nose now and is getting very aggressive. The lump has grown considerably larger over the last few weeks.

The Vet and I have been discussing his care plan more and as a family, we know we are close to the end. Paramount is his comfort and we are upping his pain medication and going on antibiotics for possible secondary infections. The biggest thing is he can't tell us how much pain he is in so I'm relying on my time as a firefighter and EMT; he's not a human, but a mammal none-the-less so similar.

I've thought ahead of when it's time to mentally prepare myself for when it's actually time to ease his pain. Problem is making the leap to that point. It's one thing to prepare in your mind but the likelihood is that the reality will be far different.

Looking back, we've accomplished almost everything on his list, just a few things left. I hesitated calling it a "doggy bucket list" because it's inevitable that as the end of the list approaches so is the end of Gunner's time with us. I've thought about it and I'm not in denial. I know what is approaching and have been preparing, but maybe it's a way to shield myself from the sadness now and the grief that is likely to come later.

Hopefully everything we have done is enough. I do take comfort that a friend of ours remarked "sometimes it's just enough that our dogs are near us." I really listened to that. Rather than think about yet more experiences, take comfort in what we have already done, in the years that we have already had him. That was a powerful lesson to learn once I saw it for what it was and understood it fully.

Lastly, know I'm torn on a lot at this stage. This is never easy and this is going to be tougher by far. How do you make the call to say enough? People say you'll know and he will let you know. Let me tell you, this time? There is a lot of unknowns here.

To say nothing of the fact that we've barely had time to grieve over Timber.

TIME IS RELENTLESS

7-10-22

GUNNER THE BEAGLE HERE

Sleeping a lot more these days, my hooman needs to sleep by me during the day now too. I want that. I don't want him to leave me during the days. The boy and girl hooman are here though and they take great care of me when my hooman is gone, but it's still not the same.

I got to have chicken most of the weekend. Tonight I got steak too! The food was nice, but I'm ever so tired these days. I ate it slowly, usually I would eat it really fast, but I can't do that anymore.

The lump hurts too. Today I was really close by my hoomans legs and I bumped into him with my sniffer. The lump really hurts and I yelped. I want the lump to go away...please make it go away hooman.

GUNNER'S PERSON HERE

Time is all that seems to matter right now. Counting it, watching it, and hoping against hope for more of it and never having enough of it. Time is relentless, it's marching on and I'm powerless to stop it. I know in my heart that is an impossible thing to do, but when it comes to Gunner, emotion wins outright over logic.

My heart is heavy, his tumor is painful. He's still happy and fine mentally, but I'm not sure of how much time is left. I know I keep saying it time and again, but the mix of emotions is what is clouding my judgment. Time again creeping into my thoughts.

I'm doing my best to manage his pain. He can't tell me if he is in pain but I know it. Accidentally bumping into each other simply reinforced what I already knew. I have to be much more careful around his tumor. I have been, but need to be even better.

Walks are be becoming more difficult for him so we take him when we feel he's up for it. Heat and humidity haven't helped lately. He is still usually able to go his route of about one mile. Nowadays we let him do what we call his "sniffy walks." Walks under none of the usual time constrains, just to let him wander. Funny there is time popping up again.

Just need to keep him comfortable as we can, but I can't imagine life without him. I've said it a thousand times and it's a thought I can't banish.

AT PEACE WITH IT

7-15-22

🐾 GUNNER THE BEAGLE HERE

I'm outside near my hoomans relaxing in the sun. I like sitting out here with them. They talk and listen to music and give me treats. I like to lay on the cool stones too. It's hard, but I like the feeling of it cooling me off. My hooman brings out a blanket? Silly hooman I don't want to lay on that, it's too hot out.

My family has been taking great care of me. I'm still eating and drinking well, but I know…I know… I'm fine with it, I have great hoomans. They have done everything they could for me. The lump...is making it hard for me to see. My sniffer hurts and my hooman gives me more medicine.

So tired, sometimes some of my medicine does that to me. Today I just want to lay outside near my hooman and sleep. I like it when he is nearby, I feel safe.

It's warm today, but not too warm. These are the days I like best. These are the days I used to dream of when the white stuff was on the ground and Bandit and I would have to huddle together to stay warm. I hope Bandit is alright. I hope he is happy with his hooman like I am with mine.

GUNNER'S PERSON HERE

Some of his symptoms are becoming more concerning. Today he woke up with another bloody nose; a sign I had been dreading. This means the cancer is spreading throughout his nose. It's obvious from the outside too. His nose is very dry and cracked. Such a cruel fate for a dog, not being able to really smell, it's the entirely of how they interact with their world.

As of now he's comfortable, but today we made the decision that it won't be long. For the last few days I've been mindful of not waiting until he has more bad days than good. I'm keenly aware of his quality of life being the most important thing. I don't want to keep holding on, keeping him in any potential pain for no other reason than not being able to let go. So far, he has more good days than bad as of late, but the signs are all there.

My guess is by early August at the latest is when we will have to put him down. The Vet and I have been talking and we want it to be before he suffers or is in too much pain. I'm torn as he is with it mentally, he's happy and eating, but the lump continues to swell. There isn't anything more that we can do. He is at his maximum for pain medication and we can't do anything about the cancer. His palliative care is coming to an end.

Just have to take each day as it comes and be at peace with it.

A SONG TO REMEMBER

7-17-22

GUNNER THE BEAGLE HERE

Having a hard time waking up today. My hooman has been giving me more of the special pills that make the lump...not hurt as much. It helps and I want to go back to sleep.

Later my hooman says we are "going for a ride in the truck." This is one of my favorite things to do with my hooman, but I'm not as excited as I usually am. The lump...is winning. I feel different, it hurts more.

My hooman is unsettled though I can tell he is really worried about me today.

He picks me up and this is usually another of my favorite things, but today it doesn't seem as fun as he puts me in the truck. I just want to curl up as we drive.

I snooze for a bit and glance over and my hooman is softly crying as we drive and singing to me softly. I like it when he does that as it makes me feel safe. I'm not sure what he is singing, but I like it when he sings to me. I know why he is crying, we won't be together much longer. The lump...is pulling us apart.

He tells me it will all be okay. I want to believe him, he's normally right, but how will it be okay if we're apart?

GUNNER'S PERSON HERE

Today was a very difficult day. My wife was working a long shift and the kids, while sad, can't really help with what I'm are going through in terms of this. I know what's approaching and can't avoid it.

I'm sad, but at peace with the decision. The great hurt of dogs is that they don't live as long as us. And each time the hurt is different. This will be the fourth time and the hardest of all.

I'll be thinking of songs I sing to Gunner when we move out west in a bit over five years. Even though I know I won't have him at that point I'll be thinking of him. For Teddy, I think of the songs that make me remember him. Seems odd to be looking ahead while he still with us, but knowing at the same time is a way coping?

He's sleeping more now and content to be near me. That's all that matters. I've done everything I can to get him to this point and don't think he'll make it to early August which was my estimate based on his symptoms. Now I don't think he has that much time.

Gunner and I went for a small walk this a.m. on the usual path he's walked countless times before. He went a little ways, but he couldn't do it. We turned around and came back. He gave me the look and I knew what it meant.

And there it hit me. I couldn't sit still, I was antsy and unsettled. I kept looking at him. The truck. That would always perk him up. Taking him outside he wasn't his usual eager self to get in. And once inside he plopped right down in the seat when usually he would have to go to the driver's side until I got in.

We just drive, where I wasn't sure, but headed out to an expressway right near the lake that is lined with trees. Windows were down and no radio, just Gunner and I with the power of silence and touch. I pet him as we drive.

Eventually we arrive at a marina and harbor of my youth. I'm not really sure why, as I haven't been here in years and I've never taken him here. Yet somehow I felt I needed to. We start to walk along the jetties as I have some vague idea of taking photos.

We sit and take some, he's happy in the sun and the photos don't quite turn out the way I want them to. They will have to do.

On the way back, it's noticeable that he is stopping to pee often, way more than normal. He is having issues with his bladder as the cancer has likely spread rapidly over the last few weeks.

My daughter's surgery is in two days. We've been working towards her surgery for almost seven years and it's been delayed over the last two due to the pandemic. We can't change it now. I have to keep him hanging on a bit more and get past this. This is heartbreaking.

Through it all he is largely himself. He wanders the park area nearby and he goes to visit almost everyone he meets. I'm concerned that he might be skittish or even aggressive due to the tumor, but he's not. He's his normal friendly self. A few people ask about his lump and I tell them. Many wish him well and feel bad for us. I'm torn as I don't want to have to keep explaining and have to keep the emotions from welling up each time. But this isn't about me. He wants to wander and I let him take me and the leash wherever he wants to go.

At least for a few brief moments, I manage a smile and stifle the tears.

DAY OF DAYS

7-21-22

GUNNER THE BEAGLE HERE

I'm really sleepy today. I'm also not really hungry anymore. I was shivering early this morning too. I got my hooman up early and he let me out, but I'm still cold. Even laying next him isn't warming me up like it usually does.

It's hard for me to sleep right now. It feels like I have to go wee-wee all the time. It hurts. How do I tell my hooman? I know he knows. He's been very concerned.

Maybe I'll just sleep here for a while longer and I'll feel better, sleeping next to my hooman usually makes me feel better.

GUNNER'S PERSON HERE

Gunner isn't acting like himself today. Since we have been sleeping on the mattress in the back I've learned to sleep lightly, as more often than not, he would have to go outside early in the morning. Around 1:30 a.m. I noticed he was shivering. It's summer and the AC is on but it's not any cooler than normal inside. I scoop him up and get him to lay next to me, he continues to shake, but eventually settles down.

Work is now messaging me—of course they are. Working in Information Technology carries certain truisms. One is you're going to be needed when you have the least amount of time. In this case over the phone instructions don't work. It's about a half hour from my house to work: get there quickly, likely fix the issue fast then go home. So about an hour of drive time and maybe ten minutes to fix. I can do that.

I get to work, fix what I need to and then head back home. Upon arrival everyone is fine. Gunner is sleeping near the table where I left him. He's breathing okay and has some towels near him.

Since my daughter was likewise sleeping and medications administered I settle in to play a few mindless video games to occupy myself. Saturday is still a few days away and he seemed settled for the moment, but that nagging feeling is there. Lately he has been content to just be nearby me and sleep. I don't want to disturb him so I let him be.

An hour later I glanced down as he startles himself and wakes up; his bladder has let go and he is wet and disoriented. I try to to get him outside and is moving slowly. He was soaked and I clean him up and carry him outside. He's shivering again. It's very warm outside and being in the sun will likely perk him up. I bring him out his water bowl, but he's so confused. Gently I coax him to drink, but he looks at it halfhearted.

He looks at me and I at him.

I find my wife and tell her "it's time, he isn't going to make it to Saturday."

FOREVER ISN'T LONG ENOUGH

7-21-22

GUNNER THE BEAGLE HERE

I'm outside and the sun is warm, the water stopped from the sky. I'm not shivering and I like that the sun is out warming me, I like it better that way.

One of the hoomans brings me an ice cream, but I really don't want it. Not hungry anymore. I'm not thirsty anymore either. I just want to lay in the grass. My snout...hurts. I look at my hooman he looks at me. My hooman is speaking on his phone thing. He's sad and crying, but says to someone "it's time to go." I know what he means. I'm ready...I can't go on like this, it's time.

GUNNER'S PERSON HERE

That call to the Vet, any dog owner who has been through it before knows the dread of this call. I've had to do it multiple times and it's never this easy. This is worse. Saturday is too far away. Gunner is not going to make it I tell the Vet, it's time and he's telling me, I can clearly see it. I really don't have to tell her more, she and I have been talking for months. The Vet agrees: it will be at 4 p.m.

Suddenly everything recedes in my life. Work, personal obligations, sports, you name it. All of it simply doesn't matter. Seemingly it was so long ago that we got him, a life time ago, forever. Now it's clear that forever isn't long enough to be with him, and endless days without him are all that are in the future. That reality that I have been pushing out of my mind for months can't be ignored any longer. I know it's here, but I don't want it to be.

We pet him gently and take some photos. It won't be long and the clock isn't stopping. Unlike with Timber where time seemed to stop waiting to take her to the Vet, for Gunner no such thing. My son comes out and pets him and we make sure to get some photos. My daughter can't as it's only two days since her surgery and is in no condition to do much.

We continue to spend time with him outside, all the while knowing time is slipping away. I want the clock to stop, for time to stand still but it won't. Mercilessly it marches on and we're powerless to stop it.

Gunner simply lays in the grass soaking up the sun and rests. He is past caring about water or food and is simply content. He's had a lot of pain medication so I hope it's done its job and he's not suffering. In this, I'm caught in the dual feelings of wanting to keep him alive and easing his pain. It doesn't make any sense.

All too quickly it's time to take him. Knowing what I have to do and what I want are two different things. And unfortunately, as a dog owner, this is one thing you have to do, you owe it to them. I lead him outside to the truck for a truck ride, except this time there is such finality to it.

UNDER THE SHADE OF A TREE

7-21-22

GUNNER THE BEAGLE HERE

Today I made the decision to leave my people, most of all my favorite hooman. I was in pain and told him, he understood. Good hooman, he always knows.

I'm not myself and the lump...hurts. I've done my best to be unafraid, but I am. I don't know what is ahead anymore and I'm scared. I'm...I'm tired of fighting too. I can't go on like this anymore.

My hooman is sad, I can tell, he's been ever so worried about me. It's okay hooman you've done your best. I love you so very much, but I can't stay any longer. I'll be brave for the both of us. I can do that one last time. You know what I've wanted for some time and now it's here. You've carried me this far, now it's my turn to carry you. You've always been by my side through this, carried me up stairs and stayed up with me for many nights when I couldn't get settled, and cared for me when I didn't feel good. Wiped the red stuff away and cleaned me up. You've worried about me so much and I can't do that to you anymore.

This last part I have to do on my own, you can't do this for me. I'm happy one last time though, the last thing I'll see in this world is you. And because of that I can leave you. I know you will be hurting and miss me, but think of all the good times we had when you are sad. It will be enough, even though it won't.

Time to lay down outside under the shade of a tree and say goodbye to you. Know that I am very sad and will miss you terribly.

Now on to my next adventure, I see a rainbow and a bridge and my paws are carrying me fast, I'm no longer in pain and am whole, except for the one person I miss very much...

GUNNER'S PERSON HERE

Despite knowing it was coming fast and that it's for the best, my heart is shattered. We had him scheduled for Saturday, July 23rd, but he told us otherwise. He made the decision for us. Once he did it was my job to carry it out for him.

It's unfair. I said (rather stupidly) when we got Gunner that however long we had him would be enough. Now time is so grossly unfair. Unfair to him most of all. Twenty years with him by my side, one hundred wouldn't be enough. Three and a half years is just not enough.

The drive was slow as the Vet is only three miles from our house. The day had some moderate to heavy showers while I was out and about, but the weather while gusty, had cleared. Gunner as he always did, was happy to be in the truck with me. He curled up right into the seat.

Pulling into the Vet I was easily able to get him out and as he always does, he wandered. I noticed though that he was more confused and meandered around the parking lot. By now his sniffer wasn't working too good.

I decided to opt for him to be outside under a tree when the time came. I've never done this before for a dog and would be doing this alone. My daughter's surgery meant someone had to be with her so I took him alone while my wife watched over her. This would only be the two of us, which in a way is fitting, but also in the same way heartbreaking.

Through tears I led him outside after completing the paperwork. At first he and I just sat under the tree with me gently petting him. Gunner in an unusual move for him simply laid down next to me and watched the comings and goings of the world. In his more spry days, he would be exploring. Now I believe, he knew and was content.

I had planned how it would be in my mind over the weeks prior as I knew we were getting closer, but Gunner, as always, had other intentions.

Scooping him into my lap he was alright for a bit until the Vet techs came out. The initial sedative shot was administered easily enough, but it took a while for him to relax. While we waited for that to fully take affect the techs who were nice enough were getting him ready for the catheter and he got stressed and yelped which he NEVER does.

No, no, no I thought this is not how I wanted it.

We agreed to take a moment and let him and I relax. They were doing great, it's not their fault but this is far harder than anytime before.

Thinking of a post I had made a few days prior about how I might remember him I started softly singing with my horrendous singing voice. As I worked my way through the song, tears began to flow stronger than before. Sobbing, heaving, angry at the same time for cancer taking my best friend from me.

He couldn't get settled. I could tell he was reacting to the sedative, but still alert. Finally he worked himself to a point he found comfortable and put his snout roughly in my hands. I pet him and told him how much I loved him and how hard this would be, but how I no longer wanted him to be in pain.

Seeing the Vet approaching I knew I couldn't drag it out this way and for him it would have to be quick. With my golden a few months back, we had a longer time to say the final goodbye when she was sedated. For Gunner that wouldn't be the case.

Like he had in March of 2020 when he had come out of anesthesia he was shaking, not unlike, he had early that morning. Sometimes those moments of clarity hit and I told the Vet: "do it quickly, don't wait." My eyes were transfixed on the needle as she injected him. No shudders and within seconds he was gone. She then softly told me "his heart has stopped."

And in those seconds my life was forever changed.

The staff quietly left me as I gently pet Gunner and cried. Cried like I hadn't before.

I apologized for all the things I did wrong, for not spending more time. You name it. I also looked at the sky and sunlight peaking through to the west from puffy clouds, tears streaming down my face knowing he was gone, knowing it, but not wanting it to be true.

He lay there, so peaceful. For once in half a year he was no longer in pain. His dry, but still soft coat and his markings I knew so well. Fortunately I was on the side away from the lump. The unwanted...thing that had robbed me of my Gunner.

I kept stroking his back and talking to him, half expecting him to perk up and look at me. But at the same time knowing what had happened and not accepting it.

The Vet comes and carries him away.

The drive home is empty. I go through the motions and pull into the driveway and that's when it really hits me: he should be at the door whining for me. He's not.

UNTIL ETERNITY

Forever

GUNNER THE BEAGLE HERE!

What's happening? I just took a nap looking into my hooman's eyes! Where is he? He was just there. Is he getting me chicken and steak? Maybe he drove away in the truck and I should go to the door and wait and cry for him! Wait a minute we weren't home, we were at a tree watching the sky.

What...what...is this place?

Never mind that...the lump...is gone! I can see and breathe again! The smells are great! I can smell things I haven't in so very long! My face doesn't itch or hurt, the hurt, the nagging pain is gone! NO MORE LUMP!

There are so many trees, flowers, and bushes for me to go wee-wee on! There are rivers and fields and the sky is blue, and warm above! The sounds are amazing and the grass under my paws is soft and squishy. The sun is warm and it's breezy, and I'm not cold, I'm not shivering. My paws are flying so fast, just like they did when I was young. Dogs, so many other dogs, time to go run and play! Aryoo!!!

This place is the best...but something is missing. The best part of me and the best part of him...my hooman where is he? Where is he? Wherever could he be? Did he leave me? Did I do something wrong? No...wait...I know, this is the place he told me of that I would go for a while till we would be together again. He would sing to me when I was hurting and made me feel better, is that what he meant when he said it would be alright?

Smart hooman, he always knows!

I hope my hooman is not hurting too much. If you see him, tell him it's okay. I'm whole. I can see and I'm alright. One day I'll see him again, but for now, it's time to run and play!

GUNNER'S PERSON HERE

I wish, I hope, I pray that Gunner is indeed happy and whole, that all his hurts are healed and he's running free with all the other dogs. I hope Sammy, Teddy, and Timber are there waiting to play with him, Teddy, of course, with the Frisbee in his mouth.

I hope, someday, I can dream about Gunner and he can tell me that he is alright and complete. That he will tell me that I've done enough, and that he forgives me for all the things I did wrong with him. I hope, that for now...he forgets me, at least just for a little while to run and play, to frolic under the warm sun and bathe in the eternal brightness of the Rainbow Bridge.

Most of all, I hope my buddy, if he does remember, doesn't miss me with the pain that is in my heart. My heart is aching here without him. But at the same time it's that heartache, that love for him that couldn't keep him here another day. I'd rather be apart from him no matter how much it hurts me, if it means he's no longer in pain and happy.

I hope that until we meet again, he's having the time of his life until eternity never parts us again.

ECHOES OF GUNNER EVERYWHERE

7-22-22

GUNNER'S PERSON HERE

This morning I woke from a deep sleep and was startled, my mind casts about for Gunner. Where is he? He's not in bed beside me. Even after putting him down, I continue to sleep on the bed on the floor of the back living room as I have for months on end it seemed. I've grown so accustomed to taking him out and only sleeping in snippets that the deep sleep has thrown me off.

"Where are you Gunner, where are you?" I call as the tears come in a torrent. I know he is gone, but my mind isn't fully processing it at that moment. Grief, overwhelming grief that feels so thick, hits me square in the face, and the realization comes to me that he is gone.

Of course he isn't here, but the echoes in my mind kept replaying that he is: that I hear his paws and nails tramping across the floor, his shuffle, almost being able to pet him. The routine of him going outside, feeding, looking for food handouts. Of him getting up at 3 a.m. and 5 a.m. to go outside. Everything just feels, and is indeed, off.

The rawness of it is so real I have to get out of the house. I can't stay here with it so quiet (my wife is at work and the kids are asleep). I go for a long bike ride and am more aware of everything as I pedal away with tears streaming down my face. I can't even listen to music, just alone with my thoughts and they are consumed by Gunner's passing. No matter how hard I try he keeps creeping back into my mind, stubbornly; like beagles often are. I knew how persistent he was in life, so it is appropriate that since we've parted, he continues to work his way into my life.

This is as it should be.

The problem, if one can call it that, is I can't get any relief, it's literally all I can think about. I head to the basement and the exercise area. I figure a karate workout will help. Nope how can I? I find it literally impossible to meditate and katas that I have known for decades? No again. I can't focus so I return to meditation and eventually, through a lot of force of will, I am able to get my mind to quiet, but only for a little while.

Still needing a respite I undertake some yard work, but again it's mindless: mowing the lawn, weeding. This isn't going to work either but power through it.

It's likely I was fooling myself into believing that I'd be able to fool myself for any length of time given that it's only been three days. That beagle stubbornness, asserts itself and gives into the fact that no matter how much I try, there is no distracting myself from the reality of him being gone.

THE SKY IS CRYING

7-24-22

GUNNER'S PERSON HERE

The rawness of Gunner's passing is oppressive, the fact of it is hovering near me. I can't escape it. He's everywhere in my life while simultaneously being nowhere. The contradiction is magnified every time we look at his and Timber's water and food bowls. We can't bear to put them away. All of the effort for Gunner's cancer meant that we didn't have time to even consider Timber or at least I didn't. And now we don't have a dog at all.

After settling down from the ride this morning, I wanted to keep busy. We had decided to plant some flowers and prepare a spot for a tree in memory of Gunner on the side of the house, but the weather decided otherwise.

In the overcast sky gentle, soft rain began to fall, matching my crying for Gunner, matching his gentle soul. Indeed the sky is crying. But just like that it stopped and the weather broke for a bit to let us finish our task.

Later that night however, the skies open up and it rained hard. It was as if the sky was angry, likewise matching some of the conflicting emotions of mine over the unfair nature of it all.

Over the next several days, the sky will be the same—some rain, some sunshine, as if it is a mirror to my feelings for Gunner. Eventually it drys out and for the next bit, no rain. As if the skies, like myself, got it all out and moved on, except I haven't.

Gunner has effected me like no other dog and the grief is likewise nothing I have ever experienced. When Teddy passed, we had Timber within days. It probably effected my relationship with her, but at the same time, didn't give me much time to grieve over

Teddy himself. That would come later, sure, but there wasn't much of a gap between the two dogs.

The rest of the day is spent watching the rain from our garage and reminiscing about Gunner, and some about Timber too. Both my wife and I are struck by how empty and still everything feels. With the two of them just the good times come to mind and very little, if any, of the bad. We also talk about the difficulty of losing two dogs within six months.

I also verbalize one of the truisms of dogs, their Yin and Yang nature. Dogs are able to give us such tremendous joy and other times soul crushing pain. That is the price one pays for being a dog owner, that someday in the future, sometimes way too soon, you'll have to face parting from them.

As we continue to chat and share a drink, the rain continues to gently fall.

PHASES OF GRIEF

7-26-22

GUNNER'S PERSON HERE

Today was the first day without the intense grief of Gunner right when I woke up. Our hearts are still shattered into a million pieces. The house is so quiet and still, we miss his presence. Today when I awoke, my thoughts went to him first and I reached down to my left side to pet him but stopped knowing he wasn't there. I stayed there for a bit just running things through my mind, wondering if I should have put him down sooner, did I wait too long? Most of all missing him.

We called him my barnacle. Everywhere I went, he went too. I couldn't even take a shower without him peeking in to make sure I was really there. Bathroom? He'd have to follow me in. Outside? Inside? Didn't mater all he wanted was to be near me. Sometimes it would get a bit much, but there isn't anything I wouldn't give for just one more second of it. And now it's gone and I find I'm missing it more than I thought possible.

That is what loss does to you, you don't really realize what you have till it's gone. Cliched? A song? Yes, but it's accurate. At the same time, I'm unsure if that was the case for me due to us being inseparable.

WE CALLED HIM MY BARNACLE. EVERYWHERE I WENT, HE WENT TOO.

I have a photo of just him and I at the Vet by a tree. I took it with mixed feelings knowing what happened 30 minutes later. In a way I felt guilty, but also wanted a photo of our last moments together.

Surprisingly the photo doesn't make me sad or grief stricken. Looking at it gives me some comfort knowing I did everything I could, and until the end, I had to put aside what I wanted. Despite it only being five days prior, I replay in my mind what I was thinking, what was coming. In the photo he is sitting there just watching the world. Did he know? Was he fine with it? A friend of mine remarked that he seemed at peace and serene. I can't see that in the photo right now. I know it is there but I'm still too deep in grief to appreciate the sentiment or see Gunner for what he was and feeling at the point.

I've had to put down dogs before, but the only word I can think of is lost. This has been far harder than any before. Part of me is missing and sure, in time, it will heal just like it has in the past. While true, that doesn't help now.

Pain is something that life is about. The loss of a dog is a pain that is unlike any other. The same friend who remarked about the serene nature of Gunner hasn't had dogs in decades. As he has told me before, he can't do it again because it's too painful. Right about now I can see the wisdom of that stance.

THE UNFAIRNESS OF IT ALL

7-30-22

GUNNER'S PERSON HERE

As I eat breakfast this morning, my thoughts turn of course to Gunner, about how he should be here and looking for dropped food. He never begged, but learned every once in a while food might just land nearby. Now of course some would "accidentally" fall...

My mind turns to the lump...adenocarcinoma. It initially presented itself as small bump on the right side of his snout, somewhat close to the eye. The truly insidious thing is that not every dog gets cancer and out of those that do? Roughly 1% will get nasal cancer. Add to this beagles are not predisposed to this type of cancer. And when I say insidious? It's because to a dog everything is a smell, it's how they explore their world in ways our sense of smell can't. The way I think about it is if a human got ocular cancer and lost their sight how devastating that would be.

Looking back on it now, with the benefit of hindsight, I don't regret the decision to keep him comfortable and opt for palliative care. He was coming up on fourteen years old when he got diagnosed and the last surgery on his left eye the year prior gave me pause. While he did make it through that previous surgery, other factors were not on his side and one year older.

The final part, the consideration and the most heartbreaking was even with surgery, chemotherapy, and radiation he might get some time to his life. Dogs sometimes get up to twenty months its been reported, but there is no curing it. By the time the lump presents itself, it's already too late. With that in mind, I had to make the tough decision to balance quality of life with the time we had left, however short vs treatment that he might not survive at his age.

While not regretting the decision is one thing, justifying it to yourself after the fact is a whole different proposition. I wrestled with my thoughts on many a night leading up to and after his passing on whether or not I took the right course of action, whether or not I chose wrong. I've also grappled with the thought (however dubious) of "my actions led to his passing." It's not an accurate statement, but part of the gamut of emotions that losing a dog generates, at least it did for me. It's part of the spectrum of grief as I experienced it. I could have saved him at least for a little while, why didn't I do it? I'm no fan of guilt and think it's largely useless, but there it inserts itself into my thoughts.

The overall fact is that I can't reconcile the unfairness of it all. His life wasn't great from what we understood prior to us. And to have it cut short by cancer that was so unlikely makes it even worse. Today it's hard to see the good we did for him when all I can focus on is that word again and again: unfair. People from the shelter told us how good of a life we gave him, how he won the "jackpot" with us. Doesn't seem like he won that now. I know they are right, but I can't or won't accept that right now.

Life isn't fair it's said, and it sure wasn't for Gunner which is what I'm most upset about. I can handle the pain and what comes with it in terms of loss. But for fate to do that to him? That I can't reconcile. Gunner did nothing to deserve what fate handed him. No dog deserves it, and doubly so for Gunner.

EMPTY DAYS

8-3-22

GUNNER'S PERSON HERE

Today was an exceptionally busy day at work and in my personal life. It was non-stop on the go from the moment the alarm went off. This is just as well as its kept me from dwelling too much on the enormity of the passing of Gunner, maybe from dwelling on the unfairness of it.

As one would expect this is the day that the Vet's office called: Gunner's cremated remains were ready for pickup. And just like that I was snapped back to the reality of his passing. I was far too busy to get away was my first thought. On second thought, I came to the conclusion that nothing mattered more. I quickly rearranged my schedule so I could take him home that afternoon, knowing I was going to have an equally busy evening and not caring about it at all.

I arrived at the Vet and for a moment I paused and lingered as I exited the truck. Of course my gaze was immediately drawn to the tree where we were two weeks before. The last time we saw each other and a wave of sadness washed over me.

Steeling myself for what was about to happen I went in, determined not to be a blubbering mess. I told them what I was there for and gingerly and quite reverently, the receptionist handed me the wooden box with his paw print and telling me how sorry they all were.

I took the box containing his remains and mumbled something and left. And just like upon entering my eyes went back to the tree. Hating it and at the same time glad that he got to pass under something so peaceful. And just as suddenly my thoughts are transported to the last time I saw him: he was being carried away from under that same tree. Now here he is, this little box with his ashes. We had just done this with Timber six months ago and the realization hasn't struck me like it has now.

Sitting in the truck with him felt right and wrong at the same time. Only a few weeks prior he and I were enjoying some truck rides which turned out to be our last. This was somber, to be expected, but... empty. The touch of his fur missing, just the wooden box. The joy that both of us experienced when riding around together was gone.

Pulling out of the parking lot my hand went reflexively to the spot where he would be and drove. Nothing there except the wooden box. Almost immediately I started talking to him, telling him we were returning home and that I missed him these last two weeks. That I hoped he was happy at the Bridge and to say hello to Sammy, Teddy, and Timber for me. That I was thankful he was my dog and how much I loved him.

The rest of the short ride was in silence as was common between us; him beside me as it was meant to be, but never will be again. I never really had to speak to him on our drives. We each knew in our hearts nothing needed be said. The simple power of touch between a man and his dog conveyed everything. Pulling into the driveway and taking him inside, I can only take solace in the fact that he is home.

Later that evening life got in the way again, I had obligations to attend to. Driving away from home, I glanced at the empty seat where he should be and just was an hour or so prior. I knew I had just brought him home, but there I was again staring at where he should be. Funny how life can make you think of the absence of something so profound as this in such simple terms: an empty truck seat.

A CHANCE ENCOUNTER

8-6-22

GUNNER'S PERSON HERE

It's been a little over two weeks and while the grief of losing Gunner has lessened it's been replaced with a feeling of something missing. That feeling I've had before with my previous dogs, but far more intense. Gunner is home with us on the stand with the rest of the dogs, but his presence while looming is at the same time missing.

My wife worked a long shift on this day, but senses that we all need to get out of the house for a while. We know what is missing: Gunner, sure. But we are missing the sights and sounds of dogs as well. It effects each one of us in a different way and yet the cause is the same, missing Gunner.

We pile into the truck and I have a halfhearted smile when I glance at the seat as my wife gets in. She doesn't have to say anything, she knows what I'm thinking. Once we head out, I don't think any of us rightly knows where to go, I certainly don't. I simply put the truck in drive and in no time at all we find ourselves at a pet store. Not at a pet store to buy a dog, it's way too soon for that. Rather it's a case of hoping to just meet some and pet them, take in the sights of them that is so missing from our lives. Unfortunately, the one we pick there are no dogs, nor are there any coming in or out of the store.

Undeterred, we head to another pet store but have to be mindful of my daughter. It's only been two and a half weeks since her surgery. While she is doing remarkably well, we are aware of not pushing it too much. It's just as well that we are quickly at another pet store. This time it's a big one and has a lot of dogs. We gravitate to where the smaller ones are, and sure enough, as luck would have it, there is a beagle there. She's a happy girl and wanders a bit before she catches us staring at her. I'd like to say she came over to us and all that but no. She just stared at us and wagged her tail ever so slowly before getting pounced on by the other dogs playing. She gets distracted from us and goes and plays. It's as it should be as she doesn't need people just starring at her.

But in that one moment, we're not too sad or broken up. It's a weird mixture of happiness and some longing but happy none-the-less.

It's then that the obvious dawns on me. This is the first beagle we have seen since we lost Gunner. The neighbors up the street have one and we hear her howling on occasion and it makes us smile, but this the closest we have been to one since.

All too quickly sadness rears its ugly head and I'm left to silently wonder if this was a good idea. We head for the truck and ride back home in silence, each of us lost in our own thoughts. My wife breaks the silence and says "thank you." Somehow she knew we all needed it, even if we each didn't know it ourselves.

If I ended it here, it would likely seem like nothing more than a story I made up, but it gets more unusual still. Unusual, but happy.

Each day at work I walk on my lunch and my path takes me nearby our first house where I used to walk Sammy and Teddy. It had been years since I did so, but my office moved nearby and it worked out perfectly. The weather is warm and with a nice breeze and I'm maybe ¼ of mile from my old house when I spot a beagle puppy on a tie out in a side yard, wiggly and excited to see me. I hesitate as he's by himself, but in no time at all the owner comes out and we chat. He tells his name is Max and its okay to approach him. I kneel down and pet him and all that puppy excitement can't be contained. I tell his owner of Gunner, and briefly, that I no longer have him. He can tell from my words just how much it means to pet little Max. That healing touch of a dog, just to be able to make that physical connection and it be nothing but good.

I'd like to think that Gunner whispered to Max that his hooman was hurting and go cheer him up. That part may sound contrived, but it's at moments like this that it's best to simply go with it and just believe in the sentiment.

SLEEPLESS AT 2 A.M.
8-11-22

GUNNER'S PERSON HERE

I've been awake for hours, can't sleep. Usually this is not a problem for me, hit the pillow, and I'm out. Tonight, however, is different. No matter what I try I can't get to sleep. Gunner and my other dogs keep creeping into my mind. Likely it's because it's only been three weeks today since we put him down. Sleeplessness hits at the times when you least expect it, at least it does for me.

I try to go back to sleep and it won't come to me. Tonight I'm back on the floor with the mattress where he and I were sleeping. It's not helping and maybe it's making it worse. The minutes tick by so slowly that it seems as if time really has stopped.

Lately I've been inundated with stories of dogs, the suffering of them, man's cruelty to them. I can't seem to escape it. It hurts to think of the abuse that poor dogs go through around the world and how perfect creatures they are and don't deserve it.

Then my thoughts selfishly turn to Gunner and how much I miss him. What his life was like before us and how much I feel cheated with the time we had with him. It's at this moment that I also take pause and consider just how much I'm looking at this through just my eyes and how flawed that is. Did he see his time with us differently? Sure dogs don't think of time they way we do but was it "enough" in his eyes? Or put another way I suppose, was he content?

This has been the latest part of the roller coaster of emotions with losing Gunner. I knew it was coming overall, but it comes in waves. Part of the grieving is there is no set time limit or path as to how one will feel, it's unexpected in the direction. What is unexpected is how different this has been from the times before. Perhaps it's because I'm older and Teddy has receded into the background of happy memories rather than his passing. It's possible I haven't even processed the emotions over Timber and my regrets with her. The grief this time isn't so much a straight line from step one to ten. It's more like traveling a road with a lot of dead ends. And when I back up and get back on the road I take another path, branch off from there only to hit yet another dead end of emotion or reasoning. It's frustrating.

I find myself staring at the laptop for a few moments as I finish this section and staring at the clock too. I'm trying to figure out just how I'm going to get some sleep before the alarm goes off and get through the work day. But also how can I quiet my mind enough to stop thinking about Gunner for a few hours and rest.

I rarely, if ever, remember my dreams, and to dream about Gunner would be a great respite, at least if only for a little while. I've tried to dream about Teddy for ten years and I can't no matter how hard I try. My wife dreams easily and remembers them. Since his passing she has dreamed of him and Timber. She tells me they are happy and healthy. I tell her to tell them I said hi and that I miss them.

She says they know.

FOCUSED LIKE NEVER BEFORE

8-13-22

GUNNER'S PERSON HERE

There are moments in one's life that are defining, that once reached one can never go back. Gunner's passing was one, yesterday was another. I realized it yesterday and it was reinforced today on my bike ride to clear my thoughts, although life, and perhaps the issues of my daily grind kept muscling its way to the forefront.

No one in this life owes you anything. No one. Not your family, your friends, your work, nothing, dogs of course excepted. And for too long I forgot this. With Gunner's passing my mind turned to, of all things, to a quote that I had liked for years but had forgotten.

Close to two thousand years ago Roman Emperor Marcus Aurelius, in part said: "Live each day as if it was your last." The sentiment that has been carried forward to modern times is that he's right because one day it will be your last. And with that knowledge if this is indeed your last day, how would you spend it?

For me the answer would be really simple. Of course I'd spend it with my dogs. But the echoes of this statement are much bigger, much broader in their implications, at least to me where I am right now.

For far too long I've been unhappy with where I've been going, and with Gunner's passing, I've reevaluated a lot of things. I could keep going on the path I'm on or make a change for the better. I've chosen the later. These last few weeks of my life and how I look at it will never be the same. I'm willing to risk the chance of failure to achieve something more than myself. Gunner did that to me, something I can't thank him enough for.

I'm nothing if not determined, and for too long I lost that determination. Gunner gave me that determination back. It was at this point I began to write in earnest about him and to take his passing and tell the story to hopefully effect change on a scale much bigger than I could ever dream of.

Gunner has taught me lots of things, things I thought I already knew only to realize I didn't. Dogs teach us so many lessons in so many ways that you only realize sometimes when they are no longer with us.

Gunner gave that back to me, yet another gift from him that I'm eternally grateful for. It's with this newly re-found determination that is propelling me forward to tell his story. Not only his story but mine and my journey with him through the toughest thing a dog owner will ever face: the euthanizing of your dog. No matter how many times you've had to do it before, it doesn't get any easier. To do it more than once only gives you forewarning, that's all. You know just how painful it will be.

It's with this determination that I go forward into the great unknown of becoming a writer. I become a writer not for myself, nor could I ever in a million years envision myself becoming one prior. I realize it's to do justice to Gunner's story and bring some good to the world through his passing. I owe him that for everything he has given to me.

WITHOUT OUR DOGS

8-16-22

GUNNER'S PERSON HERE

My wife and I have been talking about the loss of Gunner and now more freely about Timber. She has remarked about how this is the longest we have gone in twenty years without a dog. "Dog-less" is what she calls it, not dog free, which has a negative connotation to it. Thinking about it is so strange: without a dog. For us, our house, it's so bizarre to not have dog in our lives currently.

There is no right amount of time to get another dog, or not to get another one at all. We certainly don't have any answers this time around.

GUNNER HAD OTHER IDEAS

In the space of six months we went from two dogs to none. The void is something that is hard to comprehend. For years our lives were governed by the cycle of the dogs: feeding in a.m. letting outside, p.m. feeding, walks, play, and so on. Now it's gone. There is a palpable stillness and sense of something missing.

We talk about the dogs often, of my regrets with Timber. We talk about how my wife was the one who found Gunner and hoped he would be her dog. She was drawn to his smiling face and wondered how on Earth could no one have not picked him up. She was right and wrong at the same time. Right in that we would be the ones to pick him up, but wrong that he would be hers. Gunner had other ideas.

We also talk freely about the slight jealously that Gunner's attachment to me generated. It's not something I can explain. It's not that I was the one giving him extra treats (that was her and the kids) or letting him on the couch (again them). For some reason he was drawn to me and he wasn't going to be dissuaded.

I'm fairly certain that is why being dog-less is so difficult right now.

My daughter, especially, has understood this best as she and I are a lot alike. When I wasn't around, he would seek her out and be near her. She gets the hurt I feel now. Not that my wife and son don't but their relationships with Gunner were different. Not bad, just different.

We return to talking about the fact that we know we'll get another dog at some point. Or will we? The pain of losing Gunner has been a toil on all of us. Far more so than any other dog, Gunner has left an indelible mark, one that will be hard to overcome.

FIND IT IN YOUR HEART

Forever

GUNNER THE BEAGLE HERE!

I'm not sure how long it's been, time has no meaning here! It's always perfect, no white stuff on the ground! Days and nights are never cold and always warm!

I get to run and play with lots of dogs! The Rainbow Bridge is so much fun! My hooman's other dogs are all here and we sleep in a dog pile at night: Sammy, Teddy, Timber, and me, Gunner! I know Timber best of all, but I like the other two. Sammy is sort of quiet and Teddy loves to play fetch, I don't get that.

I've been talking with them and they know too, my...our hooman is still very sad. We know sometimes he cries about me just like he cried over them. I never thought about that...that there were other dogs before me.

The last time I saw him he was so very sad and told me just how much he would miss me. He told the others that too. The last thing I saw was his face, so sad and heartbroken, the others saw that too.

My hooman...our hooman is still hurting, I know it. I don't want him to continue to be sad without me. Sometimes I hear his whispers on the wind at night when the others are asleep. He says all he wants is me and wishes I could come back. But I can't. So I tell him, like when I used to wait at the door and he knew what I was saying from far away, I can't come back, as much as I might want to. I use my doggy powers to tell him he has to do one last thing for me, he has to let the pain of me go. I love him too much for him to keep suffering and in doing so find a new dog. He won't be like me and that's okay. I wasn't like Timber who wasn't like Teddy before her or like Sammy. We're all different.

But the one thing that makes us the same? Our love for you, our hooman, our friend. We miss you and will see you someday, but not now. Until then, make room in your heart for another dog just like you did for me. And if he comes from a shelter, even better. Do that for me too. I'm sad without you, but more sad that you are hurting so much.

You know deep down only a dog can help with what hurts, and if you do, do it for me, your barnacle. I say it all the time and you know it's true, my hooman knows best!

Time you knew it too.

Epilogue-

HOW DO YOU HEAL A BROKEN HEART?

September 2022

GUNNER'S PERSON HERE

It's taken a while, but I'm finally at a place of acceptance with the loss of Gunner, not at peace with it but knowing I can't change it. I hesitate to use the word acceptance as I knew his fate from the moment the Vet told me. Perhaps I'm looking at it all wrong and the stages of grief do apply. I'm ambivalent about that too. Sure there has been some of that applied, there also has been some that I haven't. For instance, there was never really a time I was bargaining that I can think of. The main thing is from the beginning of his diagnosis I knew what it meant. There was no curing him, it was a death sentence. There was no escaping it. That might sound overly harsh, but I've always been a realist. I knew what it meant and no wishing it away was going to do otherwise.

Possibly the best way to say it is I'm not hurting as badly now. It's said that a broken heart never heals, it just stops hurting as much. That, of course, doesn't help as it's here and now. The hurt over the other dogs eventually receded, but this has been far and away the worst with Gunner.

I miss Gunner terribly, every day, but like all other hurts the intensity has lessened. I still ache for him, but I'm filled with more happy than sad most days. I try to focus on the good things, but still catch myself looking to where he should be. That has been one of the toughest things for me that I can't escape: the places he should be in our lives, me in particular. Due to him being my "barnacle" nearly every where I go in the house has some meaning, some memory. Take for instance as I type this, I'm glancing over to his bed where he should be, where we spent many years of his life together. Me puttering doing something, him just wanting to be close by usually sleeping with all four paws in the air as content as could be.

I can never replace him, there will never be another Gunner the beagle for me, there never can be. Despite it all I'm hopeful because I know he'll be with me to the end of my days. I'm hopeful because no matter what, I loved him with all my heart and soul, he was and is my buddy. I hope when my time comes, he is there with the rest of the pack.

I've reflected a lot on his life and never doubted the wisdom of saying this and my wife agrees. Even if we knew what we know now, with how relatively short a period of time we would have with him, we would do it all over again in a second and that is in spite of the heartache and pain we feel now. We would not give it a second thought. He was that important and meaningful to us.

Now that he is gone? There isn't anything I wouldn't give up to have just one more day, or one more hour with him. To let him snack, to ride in a truck with him or simply just to pet him again.

As the weeks and months pass by, I'm mindful of the teachings of dogs. Dogs teach us a lot of things, Gunner taught or at least reminded me of those things and what truly matters in life. Someone decided that he wasn't worth it at over ten years old and surrendered him. And because they did, they enriched my life far beyond words, and likewise made Gunner whole. He was loved. But what he had to go through or endure to get to us? Was it worth it for him?

He came to us as a senior dog and closer to the end of his life than the beginning. I think that is why people shy away from older dogs: to protect themselves. They likely never stop and think that senior dogs need someone, even more than other dogs. If it wasn't us, would anyone have adopted him? We were the only ones who came to see him. In that, I count myself lucky beyond measure that we did.

In terms of other lessons, I learned from Gunner in numerous ways. The first of which was resilience. Did he realize the unending situation of being in a kennel through the years? I'd like to think not. Was he hungry? Beagles are food driven and then there was Gunner. When we first got him he was non-stop looking for food. If he had to resort to other means to eat? I'd rather not think about that as there is no way for me to know for sure.

Gunner also taught me a great lesson in unconditional love. Dogs want nothing from us in terms of their own wants and give of themselves. It's said that "dogs are the only thing that love you more than they love themselves." With Gunner, it was entirely accurate, yes he loved food, yet he loved me more.

But through it all he came to us as gentle of a soul as one could find. At the same time, there was always this standoffish quality to him. I don't think he ever had much interaction with people in the way of touch. Eventually, he would accept being pet and would flop on his back to get his belly rubbed, but it wasn't his first instinct to do so.

One of Gunner's most important lessons he taught me was time. Time is relentless. We're never going to get more of it and we have less and less of it as the years go by. Yet all too often we take it for granted, "there will be time" or "I'll do it later." No, no you might not. Time has a funny way of tripping up plans. I had hoped that I would have Gunner for years to come. I hoped he make it to sixteen or seventeen and spend almost all his days sleeping, only to perk up for a bit and then go back to sleep. Those hopes and dreams weren't meant to be.

Something else that I had to work through was just how much I viewed this situation selfishly. That at points I should have been looking at it from Gunner's perspective or that of my family. That through the grieving process how much I keep thinking selfishly of my loss. How "I" don't have Gunner anymore, rather than Gunner and how he saw and viewed things. It's a hard thing to articulate except to say how selfish it feels at times. It's likely not a reasonable feeling, but no one said anything about grieving over a pet is reasonable. When one really thinks about it we humanize them so much that it's too easy to get reductive and say "we're only talking about a dog."

The issue, as I alluded to in the very beginning of this book, a dog is not like any other animal on the planet. I truly believe that for all the reasons I outlined. Because of their very nature and their history with us the bonds can become exceptionally strong. I thought I had that with my Golden Retriever Teddy. With the benefit of hindsight he was everyone's dog, I was simply first among equals. Gunner, on the other hand, attached to me early and never let go. That bond was and is stronger than anything I've ever experienced with a dog. It's also the reason why this book has been so difficult to write.

Some people might scoff, even after reading this book and say "it's just a dog."

No.

He wasn't an "it" or "just a dog" he was an amazing beagle who's name was Gunner.

He was my dog and I his person. And to me and to all who met him, Gunner mattered. Gunner mattered a lot and his life taught a great deal in his all too short time with us. But the biggest, greatest thing he showed me was how much he loved me, and I in turn loved him. I never expected that I would bond with him so strongly, but I did.

I don't know what the future brings, other dogs, you name it, but Gunner will be a part of me till the end of my days.

And, I wouldn't want it any other way.

Mark T. Harter

September 2022

ACKNOWLEDGMENTS

TO GUNNER

First and foremost, to my beloved Gunner. You taught me more than I ever realized, and for that I'm eternally grateful. Most of all, you taught me bravery in the face of adversity, to continue to be hopeful. Without you, I literally would have never gone on this journey.

TO TRACY

Next, I want to thank my wife Tracy who has always been with me and comforted me through the saddest moments and encouraged me onward. We've shed tears over Gunner, sometimes happy, sometimes sad, but always with love for him and never a single regret.

You have not only been the glue that has held the family together, but the first reader of this book; I hope I did our story with Gunner justice. My first editor, the first person to encourage, the last to criticize, and always pushing me forward.

Not only all of that, you were the first person to read this, seeing as how you lived it right along with me. You are the only one who truly understood what I went through.

TO ALL MY DOGS

To all of them, however long it's been: Sammy, Teddy, and Timber. In each case, we've loved and lost you all in sadness, sometimes with hope in others devastating loss at the circumstances. I miss you all and look forward to the day when the pack is all together again.

TO MY LISTENERS

To all those however short the time that I talked about this idea to, no matter how crazy my ramblings may have seemed, thank you one and all for tolerating it. Sometimes just the smallest word of encouragement helped me move forward when I didn't want to write, when I was too sad or overwhelmed to do so. Those words made all the difference in the world and more than you'll ever know. A special thanks to Kristen Farrell who's sage insight helped me consider and allow myself some leniency when I became disheartened and refocus on the bigger picture.

TO MY DESIGNER

Daryl Corbett, the ease at which you translated my vision to the final form of the book is nothing short of extraordinary. Time and again you honed in what the look and feel of the book should be and your suggestions and creativity led it to an even better outcome.

TO MY ADVANCE READERS

I cannot begin to thank you enough for toughing it out through a difficult topic like this and your feedback. Without Corinna Capron, Kristen Farrell, Sean Maxwell, Scott Fien, and Tracy Harter this book wouldn't be in the form it's in now.

TO MY EDITING TEAM

Andrea Hicks for editing and Lauren Manuse for proofreading. Your patience in helping correct the text from an idea to a readable form was invaluable and appreciated beyond measure.

TO
GUNNER TILL
THE END OF
DAYS

Made in United States
North Haven, CT
23 June 2023

38078723R00091